# The
# LIVE
# LIFE
# NOW

## LIST

## Plan and Live Your Best Life—
## *Starting Today!*

**AUSTA SOMVICHIAN-CLAUSEN**

**ADAMS MEDIA**
New York  London  Toronto  Sydney  New Delhi

**A**adamsmedia

Adams Media
An Imprint of Simon & Schuster, Inc.
100 Technology Center Drive
Stoughton, Massachusetts 02072

First Adams Media hardcover edition
May 2022

ADAMS MEDIA and colophon are
trademarks of Simon & Schuster.

For information about special discounts for
bulk purchases, please contact Simon &
Schuster Special Sales at 1-866-506-1949
or business@simonandschuster.com.

The Simon & Schuster Speakers Bureau can
bring authors to your live event. For more
information or to book an event contact
the Simon & Schuster Speakers Bureau at
1-866-248-3049 or visit our website at
www.simonspeakers.com.

Interior design by Priscilla Yuen
Interior images © 123RF/Algirdas
Urbonavicius; Getty Images/Angelina
Bambina, Color_life, mountainbrothers,
Nataliia Prachova, ONYXprj, R-DESIGN,
robuart, siraanamwong, Vector, yganko;
Simon & Schuster, Inc.

Manufactured in the United States
of America

1 2022

Library of Congress Cataloging-in-
Publication Data
Names: Somvichian-Clausen, Austa, author.
Title: The live life now list / Austa
Somvichian-Clausen.
Description: First Adams Media hardcover
edition. | Stoughton, Massachusetts: Adams
Media, 2022 | Includes index.
Identifiers: LCCN 2021056849 |
ISBN 9781507217979 (hc) |
ISBN 9781507217986 (ebook)
Subjects: LCSH: Family recreation. |
Recreation. | Amusements. | Social
interaction. | BISAC: SELF-HELP /
Personal Growth / Happiness | FAMILY &
RELATIONSHIPS / Friendship
Classification: LCC GV182.8 .S655 2022 |
DDC 790--dc23/eng/20211207
LC record available at
https://lccn.loc.gov/2021056849

ISBN 978-1-5072-1797-9
ISBN 978-1-5072-1798-6 (ebook)

# CONTENTS

*Introduction ... 11*

**CHAPTER 4**

# Plan a More Creative Date Night ........................... 69

## CHAPTER 5
## Reconnect with Your Family ..89

# INTRODUCTION

## "What should we do today?"

It seems like a simple question, but it's one that can send you into a tail-spin! It is so easy to get lost in the "should-dos," like running errands or ticking items off your never-ending to-do list, that it can be tough to prioritize the things that really matter—deepening connections, finding joy, and experiencing life to the fullest.

Don't waste any more time thinking about what you *should* be doing. Get out there and make time for the things that mean the most to you! After all, *now* is the time to give yourself that much-needed (and well-deserved!) love, fun, and social time. *Today* is the day to take that leap, connect with a friend, and do something you may remember forever. And this book is going to be the guidance you need to make those dreams a reality!

Throughout *The Live Life Now List*, you'll find more than three hundred activities that will help you deepen your connections with others, strengthen your relationship with your partner, reconnect with a long-lost friend or relative, and more, with ideas like:

- ✓ Having your closest friends over for a themed cocktail night
- ✓ Switching up date night with your partner by skipping dinner and heading straight for dessert
- ✓ Getting the family together for a wild afternoon of backyard Beer Olympics
- ✓ Choosing a new neighborhood to act like a tourist in
- ✓ Hosting a murder mystery party

No matter what lights you up, whether it's a simple hang at the park or the adrenaline rush that comes from jumping out of a plane, this book has you covered. And once you've completed an activity, you can finish it off with a satisfying check mark next to the entry you choose.

However you decide to make your way through these pages is totally up to you. No need to read it front to back like a normal book. For instance, if you've been struggling to find approachable and enjoyable ways to reconnect with members of your family—skip right to Chapter 5!

There's also plenty of room for you to add some inspiration of your own, should you want to. Throughout the book, you'll find areas of blank journaling space to use however your heart desires: Add new activities that you think of while reading; jot down notes on how you'd like to personalize an activity for your own social life; recap how it went trying out an activity IRL; or just draw some doodles.

Regardless of how you use the book, it's here to act as that little push you may need to get back out there and experience the world in a more meaningful way and to reclaim your free time in the best way possible.

So let's raise a glass to your newly found *joie de vivre*, and get to living your life...*now*!

# CHAPTER 1

# Explore
# Your Area

There's a certain thrill to traveling to distant destinations, but don't forget about the possibilities of backyard travel, either. Sometimes all it takes is a mindset shift to see your own town with fresh eyes.

This chapter is here to help you open yourself up to the opportunities all around you, with tons of helpful suggestions on how to explore your own city or town, engage with your friends and loved ones in interesting new ways, and love and appreciate this place you call home.

Rather than heading to the same place for brunch this weekend, why not head to the park for a picnic with your friends? If you've been looking to spice up your weekdays, maybe it's time to try something new, like working from hotel lobbies around town, finding a new route on your way home from the office, or taking the initiative on planning some happy hours or lunch dates with your colleagues. These are just a few ways you can unlock the potential of your own area. Now get out and explore!

## Set Up Morning Coffee Dates

It's all too easy to fall into the rut of starting your day by rolling out of bed, chugging your first cup of coffee, and cracking open your laptop—especially if you have a hard time with work-life balance! Instead, start your day with fresh air and conversation by

setting up morning coffee dates with your friends. Whether you've been meaning to check out a new café down the street or you're bringing your own travel mugs for a walk in the park, morning meet-ups are an easy way to fit more friend time into your busy schedule and wake your brain and body up for a better day ahead.

## Choose an Area and Act Like a Tourist

There are certain activities that locals leave to the tourists. The truth, though, is that there's a reason tourists enjoy doing them. Sure, it can feel cheesy, but it turns into major fun when you bring friends along and fully lean in to the trope. Hop on a cable car, ride a sightseeing bus, breeze along on the ferry—whatever your city offers. By the end of the day, you'll have learned more about your own city and had a lot of laughs along the way.

## Gather Friends Together for an Afternoon Picnic

You know that park you always walk by on your usual route? You may not have thought about it, but that park can serve as a lunch spot. Not only are park picnics a great way to take in some fresh air; they don't require a reservation and have no time limits on how long you can stay (unless the sun starts to dip).

### HOW IT WORKS

On a sunny weekend afternoon, grab some friends and walk over to your local market to gather some food to enjoy in the park. Great options include a charcuterie board, chips, finger sandwiches, and fresh fruit. Don't forget to bring an ample amount of water and a few other fun beverages. Entertainment options are also a must, like a deck of cards, books to read, and a portable speaker.

## Accompany Your Dog-Owning Friends to the Dog Park

Who says you have to have a dog in order to take advantage of the dog park? Petting friendly canines has actually been scientifically proven to be good for your mental health, which is more than enough reason to set up a date with your friend who just got that cute new puppy. Some parks even allow pups to run around sans leash at certain hours of the morning or night, making a trip to your local dog park the best way to start or cap off your day. Grab some coffees and then make your way to the closest green space together, letting Fido play while you catch up.

## Take a Guided Tour Around Town

Taking a walking tour around your neighborhood is a great way to learn facts about its history and to get the insider scoop on interesting touch points around town. If you have friends and family who don't live close by, invite them to come visit you for a weekend and do the tour together. It's fun to share the places you love with the people you love, and it'll give you an opportunity to get amped about your area all over again, regardless of how long you've been living there.

### BONUS TIP

For extra fun, try a tour with a theme. Depending on where you are, there are a plethora of interesting options: celeb-spotting tours, nighttime ghost tours, or one that focuses on the location's unique architecture.

## Print Out a Map and Let Your Friends Circle Their Favorite Spots

You no doubt have a map application on your phone that makes it easy to find your way around, but there's still something to be said about an old-fashioned printed map. This activity is perfect for someone who just moved into town, and it's a fun way to bring your friends together to learn about your new area.

### HOW IT WORKS

The first step is purchasing or printing a map of your city. Next, have each of your friends circle one of their favorite spots in town. Create an itinerary that hits all the locations highlighted on the map, or pick just one and then use the rest of your friends' picks as a guide for what to do together the next couple of weekends.

## Bring a Camera with You on a Walk (and Leave Your Phone)

Explore your area without even leaving the neighborhood—it's all about perspective, anyway. Next time you plan on taking a stroll around with a friend, try leaving your phones at home and bring your cameras instead, whether that means an old point-and-shoot from 2005, a Polaroid, or a DSLR. Stop and take the time to photograph things you hadn't noticed before: fun signs, art, interesting people, flowers in bloom. Afterward, head over to a café or your place and compare your findings. You'll be shocked at how different your photos ended up, which is the fun of photography. If you're looking for some new art to put on your walls, have your favorites printed and put in fun frames.

## Meet Up with a Friend in Their Neighborhood

Have a friend who lives across town and who you usually meet somewhere in the middle? It may be time to hop on the subway and make your way over to their neighborhood for a change. Not only will they be relieved that they can stay put, but you'll also get the opportunity to check out what they love about where they've put down roots. In exchange for the trip over, ask them to put together an afternoon itinerary of their favorite spots in the neighborhood, starting with their go-to breakfast or brunch spot and then moving on to shops, parks, gardens, galleries, and more. Next time, you two can switch roles.

## Plan a Community-Based Culinary Day Tour

In practically every town or city, you can find pockets of unique culture. Support your local communities by planning a day full of new food and fun, making your way through cafés and restaurants that you may have never tried before. Even better if you bring a friend who can show you the ropes!
If you're going with one other person, take turns picking which place to pop into—if you pick the breakfast spot, your friend chooses where to eat lunch.

## Pretend to Be an Influencer for the Day

See your neighborhood from a different perspective and pick up some quality *Instagram* content by getting your friends together to act like influencers for a day. Some fun photo shoot options include: inside a light-filled coffee shop with a cappuccino in your hand; in front of an iconic mural wearing your favorite outfit; on top of a parking garage or rooftop at sunset; or walking down the most charming street in town.

Photo walks can easily be found online through social media sites and forums. If you'd like to plan your own photo walk, simply take a look at a map of your area and mark down some spots known for their great photo opportunities, making note of all the cool murals, charming streets, and colorful drinks you come across.

## Try a New Route to (or from) Work

You know the quickest way to get to your office or coworking space, but taking the path less traveled can lead to unexpected new experiences or local gems to uncover. Plan your route the night before, making sure it adds at least fifteen extra minutes of unhurried commute time between your home and your destination. Then, take your time soaking in all there is to see on your new route, stopping in for coffee and a pastry at a new place, parking at a spot with a view, or meandering through a square. If you decide to take a different route home after work, you may want to share your location with a friend, spouse, or roommate, so they know when you get home safe.

## Resolve to Walk More and Take Public Transportation

If you own a car or the public transportation offerings in your area are less than stellar, it can be tempting to drive wherever you go. Instead, allow yourself more time to get from home to your destination, and challenge yourself to try getting there sans automobile. On the journey, you'll see a different side of your city and will get an even better idea how it's laid out, passing through neighborhoods you haven't explored yet and walking by new bars and restaurants to add to your list.

**BONUS TIP**

Whether your neighborhood offers a bike share program or not, it's usually pretty easy to find a bike shop in town where you can rent a set of wheels for the day. Take advantage of bike paths that allow you to see your city from a new point of view as you zip around town.

## Check Out the Local Suburban Food Offerings

Cities and downtown districts are known for their restaurants, but the suburbs are also a relatively untapped well of dining potential. That's usually where one can find the hole-in-the-wall, mom-and-pop spots that have unparalleled authenticity and flavor. Plus, they usually yield more affordable meals than you'd be able to find for the same quality in the city.

Next time you feel like venturing out for dinner, bring your foodie friends to check out an immigrant-owned spot in your closest suburb—it's guaranteed the restaurant will appreciate your business, and you'll gain a new secret spot.

## Crash an Open House (or Two)

We all have that neighborhood in our city or town—the one with über-charming, perfectly manicured streets and unique homes that we like to walk by while pointing out our favorites. Next time, play the role of potential home buyer by checking out open houses for the listings in your favorite areas. You might be able to score some free food or drinks, and you'll get the added bonus of potential interior design inspiration for your own abode. If you're actually on the hunt for a home or apartment to rent or buy, you'll get a great sense of which neighborhoods are the perfect fit for you and have listings with the most bang for your buck. Make sure to grab the contact information of the broker or Realtor at any properties you really liked.

## Subscribe to Local Newsletters

Ever feel like some people seem to know how to find the coolest openings, exhibits, and events every weekend? You can do that too. One of the best ways to get the inside scoop on the best happenings around town is to seek out the journalists, event planners, and influencers in your area and subscribe to their newsletters, read their blogs, or follow them on social media. Local digital publications are also a good source for events.

**BONUS TIP**

Keep your eye out for local newsletters that occasionally include promo codes, which will allow you to purchase tickets for a promoted event at a discounted rate or even for free. Forward the best newsletters to those friends who want to be in the know, or invite them to an upcoming event.

## Give Your Local Bands Some Love

Seeing your favorite musician or band is a whole experience—one that usually requires some major dough, intense planning, and getting friends on board. After all that, you may still end up in the nosebleed section! While occasionally worth the effort, why not skip all the fuss and find some new favorites? Tickets to small shows featuring local bands or traveling up-and-comers usually set you back the price of a single craft cocktail, and these performances often feel much more special and intimate. For a spontaneous evening out, gather a group of your friends and blind-pick a local show to check out. Some locations even offer services that take the guesswork out of picking a venue, like Sofar Sounds, which curates surprise shows in cities around the country.

## Spend the Whole Day at One Museum

When you're touring a new city, it's easy to feel overwhelmed walking into a museum—so much to see! Plus, with a limited amount of time at that destination, you can't be blamed for rushing through for the sake of experiencing more of what the area has to offer. But that's the great thing about exploring your own town or city—you can slow down the pace.

**HOW IT WORKS**

Bring your most art-appreciating friend along for the ride and start out in the morning, when the crowds are still thin. Then, make your way around at a pace that allows you to really take it all in, stopping at your favorite works to discuss them with your friend or appreciate them together silently. At peak tourist time, take advantage of the optimal people-watching opportunities.

## Set Out to Find the Best X

Are you a chocolate cake addict? A cocktail aficionado? Everyone has that one dish or drink that they order without fail when it's spotted on a restaurant menu. Instead of hoping you'll just come across it, become the local expert on where to get the best one in your area. You'll discover new restaurants you may not have visited otherwise, and you may inspire your friends to do the same with their favorite dishes. To keep track of them, create a folder in your Google Maps app where you keep a list of all the best spots in town for that particular dish.

## Attend Business Association Meetups

Sure, professional networking can be draining when it's imposed on you, but what about when you seek it out yourself? Sometimes all it takes is a slight mindset shift. Think about joining a business association or professional networking group in your area as a unique chance to make connections that could benefit not only your career but also your social life.

Keep your mind open to the possibilities as you attend happy hours and workshops all over town, discovering new spots and making new friends who share a passion for your industry.

## Work Remotely from Hotel Lobbies

If you've only been working from home or at your local café on remote days, you've been missing out on another great option: hotel lobbies. Besides providing a luxurious environment and ample seating, nicer hotels usually have free Wi-Fi available in the lobby, and many of them even have cafés attached where you can secure your caffeine fix.

**BONUS TIP**

Working from a gorgeous hotel lobby can make you feel like a tourist in your own town, and you can enhance that experience by consulting the hotel's concierge for tips on where to go and what to see in the area. You may be surprised by what they suggest.

## Discover More of Your Town's History

Learning about the background of your own city or town can lead to some fascinating discoveries—and you may end up looking at your area from a different perspective. Dive in through online research, or watch a documentary if there's one available. Next, bring your most curious friend along for the ride as you check out the historical markers on a local town hall or the house placard on the place up the street. You can point out all of the places you researched online, and the experience will give you both a richer understanding of the place you call home.

## Mark the Places You've Been with Pins

Have you ever seen a world map used as decor in a home or bar, with pins or tacks marking the places that someone has traveled? Try doing the same with a detailed map of your own city. Hang it on your wall and make note of new locations you've visited. Not only will your map look cool; it can also serve as a visual icebreaker for guests.

### BONUS TIP

Instead of just printing out a traditional map of your area from Google Images, try looking on sites like *Etsy* for ones made by local artists or vintage maps to add more of a personal flair and design touch. You can put your map in a frame and, instead of marking it up with pins, use a gold Sharpie marker to draw dots on the glass. That way, if you decide one day that you want to display the map sans markings, it'll still be fresh and unblemished.

## Explore Your City's Green Spaces

Did you know that spending time in nature has been scientifically proven to reduce stress and improve your mood? Luckily, most cities and towns have a variety of green spaces in which to take advantage of those important benefits, from public parks and botanical gardens to hiking trails and foliage-rich squares. Make it your mission to visit all the green spaces in your city, recruiting friends to come along to develop peace of mind together. Green spaces can also act as a great respite for you in the middle of your day. Next time you're having a stress-ful time at work, treat yourself to a cup of coffee and sip it in the park before you return to the office.

## Follow an Itinerary

Thanks to the number of travel websites, you don't even have to come up with your own backyard travel itineraries if you don't want to. Type in the name of where you live followed by "after-noon itinerary" or "weekend trip," and you're sure to get tons of results with fun ideas on how you can spend an amazing day in your own area. Even if you don't live in or near a major city, you'll find lots of credible bloggers with itinerary suggestions of their own, and forum sites like *Reddit* are packed with user-curated single- or multiday itineraries for almost anywhere. Pick one and follow along word for word!

## Make a Local Bucket List

Put together multiple weekends' worth of itineraries at once by making a local bucket list of all the bars, restaurants, and attractions you've been dying to check out. Once you have that list, pick a different list item for each day you'd like to spend exploring. Take a look at what other fun stuff is nearby, or invite friends who live in that area on your adventure. Fill in your day with places you can stop by before or after you tick off that bucket list item, and make sure to schedule plenty of time to simply explore.

## Set a One-Hour Rule

There's so much more to any area than just downtown. Less than an hour outside of your neighborhood, there are lots of local activities to explore, whether that takes the form of a nearby beach, mountainous hiking trails, vineyards, gardens, or other points of interest. Instead of sticking around town this weekend, take the afternoon to check out the cool offerings waiting to reveal themselves just an hour's drive or less outside your city limits. If you don't have a car, check out the trains or shuttles you can take, or ask a friend with a car to accompany you and let them know you'll contribute to the cost of gas.

## Do One New Thing Each Saturday

Sometimes it can feel like you've been "meaning to check out" a new spot in town for months now, or maybe you're kicking yourself for missing out on a museum exhibition that you realized is already over. Without a solid plan in place, these opportunities can easily pass us by as everyday life gets in the way. An easy way to prevent that from happening is to schedule one new thing to try on the same day every week, whether it's a new brunch spot you want to check out with friends or a pop-up gallery that you and your partner want to see. When you hear about fun new places to visit, add them to your "new things" calendar immediately so you won't forget about them.

## Keep Tabs on Community-Based Events

If you're feeling disconnected from your community, make an effort to participate in more events. Community means something different to everyone, so for you it might mean your local neighborhood, your religious community, or your cultural community. Community cleanups provide great opportunities for bonding with people while making your neighborhood or local nature trails cleaner places to enjoy. Neighborhood festivals and block parties are also super fun to attend. Keep an eye out for unique events that your community puts on that can't be found anywhere else. In Washington, DC, for example, international embassies often plan events that provide participants with a way to learn about and reconnect with their culture.

## Make New Friends Around Town at Meetups

Whether you're utilizing the *Meetup* website, *Instagram*, or Tik-Tok, meetups motivate you to explore different parts of town, and they help bring you out of your own social bubble. Using a website like *Meetup*, you can be at someone's house across town baking cookies one day and running around a track with a new group the next, while *Instagram* meetups are perfect for meeting people with shared interests, like photography. Apps like TikTok might not seem like the typical place to find meetup groups, but actually, a lot of people use the app to create callouts for meeting new friends. If you've just moved to a new area, try searching through the location's hashtag, or create your own video and ask people to comment or send you a message if they live in town and are looking for new connections.

## Find the Best People-Watching Spots

Chilling out and people watching is a fantastic way to spend a relaxing afternoon. It's super entertaining, and it helps keep you connected to the energy of your area.

### HOW IT WORKS

Find your favorite areas to hang out and people-watch around your city or town, like the coffee shop, the park, on a city bench, or at the waterfront. You'll be amazed at how many different kinds of people and groups you see, from businesspeople to performers, joggers to artists, and everyone in between. These people make up the fabric of where you live. Grab a friend who you've been meaning to catch up with and take turns making up backstories for the most interesting people who pass by.

## Have a Spontaneous Day

Sometimes no planning is the best planning, and that can lead to the most unexpected locations and experiences. Invite
your most spontaneous, up-for-anything
friends to spend a day with no rules, following wherever the wind ends up taking
you. Pick a starting point in an area of
town you've yet to explore fully and just
go for it, walking around and stopping
anywhere that suits you. You may end up
at a cool museum, trying a new cuisine,
or finding your new favorite clothing boutique. For this day, the city is your oyster!

## Show Your Neighborhood Off to Out-of-Towners

If you have friends and family who don't live close by, invite them
to visit you for a long weekend. Bringing them to all the tourist
sites in your town as well as some of your favorite local spots will
make your city feel brand-new to you again as you see it through
their eyes. It's fun to share the places you love with the people you
love, giving you the opportunity to get amped about your area all
over again, regardless of how long you've been living there. Your
visitors will have a blast with you as their tour guide no matter
what you end up doing, so it's a win-win situation.

# CHAPTER 2

# Become the Host(ess) with the Most(ess)

When it comes to your social life, learning how to host is one of the most fun and rewarding things you can do. There's nothing better than knowing your friends and loved ones had a great time spending the evening in your space. Gone are the days when you had to deal with going to events full of people you don't know (or don't like), because you curate the guest list!

In many ways, hosting puts the ball in your court in the best possible way. You can get creative with themes, activities, and decorations, and once you're ready to go to bed it's time for everyone to head home for the night. That's what this whole chapter is about: helping you to be the best host in town who is also having the best time.

As you read on, you'll see that there's truly no one-size-fits-all way to host, either. Inviting friends into your space doesn't mean that you have to throw a party. Hosting can take the form of anything from a clothing or book swap to a DIY trivia night, a friendly baking contest, or even PowerPoint presentations (really!).

## Throw a Themed Cocktail Night at Your Place

The grown-up version of a themed party, hosting a cocktail night is a great way to gather a small group of friends together for an evening of boozy fun and creativity. Some fun theme options might include *The Great Gatsby*–era 1920s, a tropical beach luau, a favorite movie reference like Harry Potter, or something personal to you and your friends!

Regardless of the theme, it will help encourage your friends to break out of their comfort zone and embrace new characters.

### HOW IT WORKS

Ask each of your friends to pick one signature cocktail that they'll be sharing with the group. Have them create a little presentation to share their creation. That could be a live demo, a cocktail-themed dance number, or even a funny PowerPoint...the possibilities are endless! Set the mood with decorations and entrance music for each cocktail creation, and you'll be set!

## Set Up a Brunch Potluck with a Mimosa Bar

Bottomless brunch at a restaurant is always a fun time, but when the two-hour mark is reached, it's usually time to sign the check and leave. Next time, invite friends over for brunch at your place, enticing them with a DIY mimosa or Bloody Mary bar. All you need is a table; a few carafes for fruit juices, champagne, or prosecco; and, if you want to get fancy, some bowls of garnishes like fruit, mint, and other fun drink toppers.

If you're looking to chef it up, prepare food in advance, but another option is to make it a potluck. Some friends can bring their favorite brunch dishes, while others supply extra bottles of booze.

## Get Into Character with a Murder Mystery Dinner Night

Why settle for a normal dinner party when you can spice it up with a little mystery and intrigue? Solving a hypothetical murder mystery case with your friends is a fun way to be silly and let loose, and the length of the party is up to you. Check online for lots of inventive prompts available for free or for purchase. Next, choose a story line, and then comes the fun part: picking roles for your friends.

Be sure to send your friends their designated roles with enough time for them to put together a costume and get acquainted with their character. On the night of the party, start with dinner in character before the first "murder" happens. Then it's up to you to set the pace, break out some clues, and get the drinks flowing.

## Choose a Decade Theme for Your Pregame

Everyone knows the pregame is the best part of any evening out. Make it even more fun by inviting friends to vote on a decade (or choose one yourself) to dictate the dress code for the night. Start by deciding where you'll go after spending time at your place. Karaoke, trivia night, or dancing are all great options. Next, think about what theme might be a fun addition to the vibe for the evening.

Whether you land on the funky seventies, punk nineties, or trendy Y2K, you and your guests will have a great time picking out outfits and crafting a shared playlist for the get-together. A sixties theme, for example, might mean groovy prints, bell bottoms, and flower crowns, and you can't forget to queue up songs by iconic groups like the Beatles and the Supremes.

## Hit the Farmers' Market for Dinner Party Inspiration

It can be tough cooking for a group, especially when you have no idea what to make! Get inspired for your next dinner party by visiting your local farmers' market, where you'll find beautiful, seasonal produce, crafts, and more sold by passionate purveyors. Wandering around a farmers' market is a relaxing experience, and a much more enjoyable way to get your dinner shopping done than battling crowds at the supermarket.

For your next big dinner party, pick up to three different kinds of vegetables that are calling out to you; a protein for meat eaters; and a loaf of bread and some artisan cheeses for an easy, crowd-pleasing appetizer. Suddenly, you've got yourself a fresh idea for dinner with ingredients you can feel good about purchasing.

## Skip the Bar and Plan Your Own Trivia Night

Let's face it: Sometimes the idea of going out on a Friday night sounds downright tiring. That doesn't mean you don't want to see your favorite people, though! Instead of spending money at the bar, invite some friends over for a fun trivia night. General trivia is always a good option, or if you and your friends have a collective passion, then use that as your theme. Act as the host or pick an app like *Jeopardy!* Trivia Quiz Game, which does the work for you. Don't forget to pick up a small prize to award the winner(s) at the end!

## Have Friends Bring Over Their Favorite Games

Game night with close friends is always a fun go-to for any night in. It's easy to find yourself in a board game rut, though, so if your existing game arsenal doesn't bring much excitement anymore, it's time to look at better options! The easiest way to find new games is by calling on your friends' collections, which will allow you to try out a bunch of fun games without the pressure of having to purchase.

### HOW IT WORKS

When you're sending out the invitation for this week's game night, ask them to bring over their favorite board games or to come prepared with a card game to share with the group. Inviting a small group may mean you can try out more than one game that night, or you can start a rotation with a larger group of friends. Who knows? You might even find your new favorite game in the process!

## Try Jenga Giant with a Twist

Spice up your next get-together with a game of Jenga (no, seriously!). Our favorite childhood game is cool again, and you can even find Jenga sets at some of the hippest bars and beer halls. Whether it's Jenga Giant or the classic set, break it out along with some permanent markers the next time you have friends over. Take turns writing down fun dares and questions on each block in the set, then construct your tower. As you take turns pulling out blocks, use what is written on them as your guide for what to do next. A question might be as simple as "What is your favorite travel destination?" or a dare that's a little juicier.

## Get Fancy with a Grazing Table

When hosting friends, it's natural to want to provide them with something to peck on. Say goodbye to boring chips and dip at your next function, and to bowls in general, by setting up a grazing table. First, set out wax paper in the dining room or on a coffee or console table to avoid making too much of a mess. Next, it's time to get creative by laying down cheese, crackers, fruit, honeycomb, nuts, candy, or whatever else you think your guests might want directly on the wax paper. Dress it up with sprigs of herbs or flowers, and you've got an instant party showstopper.

## Make the Most of Your Closets with a Clothing Swap

It's completely normal to break out your clothes for the upcoming season only to realize that half of the stuff no longer fits your style. Before you head over to your local Goodwill or Buffalo Exchange, invite your friends over for a clothing swap. Together, you'll pool even more pieces to donate and find new ones for your own closet without costing yourself a dime.

### HOW IT WORKS

Start by scouring your own closet with a large box nearby, tossing in items that you no longer want. A good rule: If you haven't worn it in the last year, you can probably live without it. Ask your friends to do the same. Set up stations around your living room for everyone to display their unwanted items. Next, have everyone walk around and pick up pieces from one another's piles. The next day, bring the leftovers to the closest consignment shop.

## Throw a Plus-One Party

Ready to make tons of new friends all in one night? Have people over to your place for a plus-one party, where each attendee is invited to bring one other friend that isn't already in your immediate circle. Having all those new faces at one shindig will facilitate a totally fresh vibe for the night, and you'll get the chance to meet cool people that you know your friends love too.

**BONUS TIP**

Are you single? Try throwing a singles' version of the plus-one party, inviting only friends who don't currently have partners, and spicing up the evening by asking each of your invitees to bring a single friend along with them. You'll meet lots of new, fun people vetted by your closest friends, and the other singles at the party will thank you for giving them an opportunity to make unexpected connections.

## Turn Your Home Into a Theater for Movie Night

There's movie night and then there's *movie night*. Turn yours up a notch this weekend by picking a crowd pleaser you know your friends will love, whether they're Harry Potter fans, Marvel superhero lovers, or Lord of the Rings buffs. Next, hit the party store for budget-friendly decorations that will transport your guests into the movie, and grab snacks to munch on after the show starts. Extra points for those who invest in a backyard projector and cozy beanbags for summer night showings.

## Find Your New Favorite Bottle with a DIY Wine Tasting

No vineyard, no problem when it comes to hosting an at-home wine tasting night. While one glass of good vino can cost around $15 per glass at a bar or restaurant, an entire bottle of decent wine can cost the same amount when purchased from your local wine shop. Start a wine night fund among friends, asking each to contribute a small amount of cash or bring their favorite decently priced bottle to share. Together, you'll be able to create your own tasting for way less, with way more wine to boot.

**BONUS TIP**

For those in need of a pro's advice, there are also wine tasting sessions and classes available for purchase online with bottle suggestions, so that all you have to worry about is sipping.

## Tap In to Your Inner Creative with an Art Party

The options are endless when it comes to getting creative with your friends. Whether you're interested in painting, knitting, polymer clay sculpting, or something else, all you need to gather for a good time are the base materials and some inspiration. For a fun paint-and-sip night, grab some canvas sheets, a set of acrylic paints, and some brushes from your local craft store. Stock up on a few bottles of wine too. Before your friends come over, set up stations around the table or even on the floor, if you have cushions to sit on. Create a still life in the middle using whatever you might have at home—a tablecloth, vases, fruit, flowers—and get to painting!

## Get Sweet with a Competitive Bake-Off

Do you and your friends share a major sweet tooth? Get your fix with a friendly competitive bake-off. First, pick a theme; next, set the rules and date. Choose a simple theme based on a single baked good (scones, cakes, cookies, etc.), or plan something more involved, like Afternoon Tea, All Chocolate Everything, or Seasonal Fruit. Once your friends arrive, have each competitor set up their bakes on a kitchen island or dining room table with description cards. Those who didn't participate in this round conduct a blind tasting. Voters can cast the ballots by texting you their favorite. The winner gets all the glory and the honor of picking the next theme!

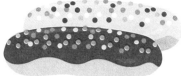

## Host an Ice Cream Social

Whether you aren't much of a drinker or you just need a night off, booze is certainly not necessary to throw a fun night in with your friends. Instead, throw it back to the days of retro ice cream parlors with an ice cream social.

### HOW IT WORKS

Hit your local thrift store for quirky glass bowls on the cheap, then the supermarket for fun toppings like whipped cream, maraschino cherries, chocolate hard shell, and rainbow sprinkles. Provide big tubs of the Neapolitan basics, or ask each friend to bring a pint of their favorite flavor for more variety. For extra fun, set a 1950s theme for the evening and ask everyone to come dressed for the occasion.

## A Black-Tie Affair in Your Living Room? Why Not?

Do you have a fancy outfit you've never had an event to wear it to? Instead of letting it collect any more dust, create your own special occasion. People might think you're extra, sure, but they'll be just as excited as you are to throw on their best duds for a fun night. Make sure to set up a photo opportunity area, decorating one wall in your place however you'd like. Extra points if you include a bucket of cheap props and an instant camera with a few packs of film. Before the party starts, grab a bottle of bubbly to pop at some point during the night, and pour it over a stacked tower of plastic coupe glasses—just for the drama of it all.

## Start a Book Club with Your Own Rules

The idea of joining a traditional book club can sound drab to some, but you and your friends can plan it your own way. Books can teach us something new, help us to live our best lives (ahem), and transport us to another time or place. Besides providing the inherent benefit of reading more, a book club also gives you a good reason to see friends on a regular basis. Take turns picking books that sound exciting, intriguing, or even sexy, then have your friends over for a low-key chat about your impressions. If one of your friends forgot to read the book that month, no problem—they get to provide the snacks and beverages to make up for it.

**BONUS TIP**

If you and your friends aren't big readers, try the same idea with podcasts, audiobooks, or magazine articles.

## Plan a Grown-Up Slumber Party

We all get tired from time to time of doing exclusively adult things, and that's okay. Break free from a rut and reinvite fun into your life by having your friends over for some good old-fashioned bonding time. Wearing pajamas is always encouraged at these kinds of functions, as is building a living room fort and kicking a ball around outside or painting each other's nails. Try going the whole night without phones so you won't feel obligated to check your email or document the whole experience for social media. The time will fly by as you watch movies, swap funny stories, and sip wine. The next morning, coffee and pancakes mark a perfect ending to the festivities!

## Become Amateur Iron Chefs with an At-Home Cooking Contest

Bring out the competitive side in your friends with a little cooking competition. Act as the host for the evening, and ask a couple of guests with discerning palates to serve on the judging panel. Pick the theme at least a week ahead of time to let your "contestants" prepare, then watch it go down battle royale–style right there in your own kitchen. Hand the winner a prize of your choosing at the end of the night, whether it's the right to choose the next theme, an actual trophy, or a bottle of booze.

## Set Up a Neighborhood Scavenger Hunt

Want to get to know more of the people who live in your immediate vicinity? Start by posting about the idea in your neighborhood chat group if you have one (and if you don't have one, maybe this is a good time to start it yourself!). Those who are interested may even be willing to help you plan it. Next, pick a theme and start searching for fun landmarks, writing riddles, and picking small prizes to hide around the neighborhood. Kids and adults alike will love ticking off boxes as they make their way through the checklist, and you'll get to make new friends who live close by.

## Start a Monthly Potluck Club

If you've been working on your cooking skills lately, here's the perfect chance to share your new favorite dishes with your friends. Not everyone may want to prepare a dish every month, so cast a wide net, sending out a group text explaining that only five or so dishes need to be made for each meeting of your potluck club. Once the theme of the month has been settled on (a few good ideas include creative sushi iterations, kitchen sink meals, or international takes on American classics), send your group a callout for submissions. You'll all have fun getting creative with your dishes and laughing together about less-than-successful attempts.

## Get Silly with an Ugly Sweater (or T-Shirt) Party

We all know that ugly sweater parties are the best, and they don't have to be relegated to the holiday season. The fun of an ugly sweater party is in its pure silliness, which you don't even need a sweater for. Just pick an article of clothing that you want guests to get creative with, whether that takes the form of cheesy thrift T-shirts, statement socks, or bold wigs. The idea is that everyone is wearing an icebreaker piece that prompts conversation and laughter. For extra fun, bring your group out to the bar after you're done pregaming at home. It's guaranteed you'll be the most popular people there that night—a chance to make even more new friends.

## Indulge In a Relaxing Spa Day (or Night) with Your Friends

Hosting all of these fun social events can get tiring, and everyone needs to indulge in a little self-care from time to time. Instead of having people over to party this weekend, switch up the programming with a DIY spa day. Ask your friends to come over in their comfiest outfits, and plan on relaxing together. Have a package of face wipes on hand in case anyone shows up in their makeup. Indulge in sheet masks and healthy finger foods like crudités. A jug of cucumber water on the table and a crowd-pleaser movie in the background will complete the mood.

**BONUS TIP**

If you plan on having people over during the morning or afternoon, you can also ask your guests who would be interested in a relaxing yoga or meditation session. Those who want to get their yoga on can bring their own mats.

## Gamble for Treats at Poker Night

Poker nights can be fun, but intense competition can make the whole affair a little tense. Loosen it up a bit by taking money out of the equation, opting instead for winners to take home less consequential prizes like lollipops, chocolate coins, or cans of beer. You and your friends will have just as much fun sizing each other up from across the table, and those who don't come out victorious won't have to leave extra bummed about losing cash. If you want to be super extra, buy some cheap trophies online or at your local party store, and write the winner's name on it at the end of the night.

## Host a Karaoke Night

Hitting the town for karaoke night is always a good time, but unless your town or city has the kind of karaoke bars with private rooms you could be subjecting yourselves to long wait times and listening to terrible singers who aren't your friends. When you host your own karaoke night, there are no wait times, and karaoke microphones that connect to mobile applications are surprisingly affordable. That's pretty much all you and your friends need to "release your inhibitions" to Natasha Bedingfield classics or share your hidden rap skills.

## Get All Your Friends' Pets Together for a Pooch Party

The only thing better than having a dog in your house is having six of them, which you could actually make a reality by inviting your friends and their pets over for a puppy soiree. Make sure you clear with your guests beforehand that their dog is housebroken and sociable, so that everyone feels comfortable (and so that you don't end up with pee on your rug). Otherwise, just make sure to provide hydration and treats for both your human and canine visitors, and get ready for some pretty amazing photo ops.

**BONUS TIP**

You can even set up photo stations around the house, which is easy to do. For example, set up a string of fairy lights underneath clouds made of cotton stuffing, or if it's autumn you can use the wheelbarrow in your garden and place some pumpkins and flowers around it.

## Help Your Friends Spark Joy, Marie Kondo–Style

It can feel overwhelming to get back into a social routine when your home base is a mess, and if you're feeling that way, there's a good chance that some of your friends are too. Help each other out and eliminate the monotony of chores by getting together for organization afternoons, rotating to a different friend's place every time you meet up. Your friends can help you pick what "sparks joy" in your home and what may be better to toss. It's a win-win to end with a clean home and an even squeakier conscience, knowing that you added points to your karma bank for helping out a friend in need.

## Diversify Your Houseplant Collection with a Propagation Swap

Whether your pothos vines are starting to drag on the ground or your succulent collection has taken over every windowsill in your home, most serious plant parents know deep down they could probably benefit from pruning their babies back once in a while. Those same indoor-greenery lovers also know that once you get started, it's nearly impossible to stop collecting new plants, and a propagation swap is the most cost-effective way to get your hands on new varieties.

Invite only as many friends as you're willing to clip cuttings for, then ask them to do the same from their plants and bring them over. In an instant, you'll gain several new species to proudly display in your home. If you're feeling really generous, hit the thrift store beforehand to search for tiny vessels in which to send your clippings home with friends.

## Host Your Own Backyard Games

Take a cue from your favorite beer hall or
outdoor bar by having a group over for
an afternoon of backyard games. Classic
options like cornhole and horseshoes are
always fun, or you could throw it back to
your college days with a long table and
some red Solo cups. Beer pong, flip cup,
and slap cup are all fun games that help
amp up the energy of the party and promote camaraderie among guests. If your

goal is to bring a feeling of teamwork to your gathering, you can
even facilitate activities like a wheelbarrow race, a water balloon
toss, or tug of war.

## Have People over for Puzzle Night

Though a game night can lead to competition among friends, a
puzzle night can do the opposite: facilitate a calm teamwork mentality. Next time you and your group need a chill night in, a puzzle night is the perfect option. Just clear enough space around
your dining room or coffee table, set out some snacks, and put on
a classic movie to play in the background. You'll all have a great
time sitting around chatting and completing the puzzle together.
Assemble your puzzle on a puzzle board in case you don't finish in
one night, or you'd like to frame it later.

## Gather with Your Neighbors in a Communal Space

One of the easiest ways to connect with your neighbors is by taking advantage of any kind of communal space that's available. If you live in an apartment building, this might come in the form of a shared rooftop, patio, or clubhouse, all of which are usually underutilized. Those who live in a more traditional neighborhood may have a park close by, and condo communities usually have a shared green space. Regardless of whether you just moved in or not, invite some of your neighbors for a casual hangout in one of these spaces. If you don't know any of them yet, hang out there on your own and make conversation with those coming in and out.

## Coordinate a Networking Soiree

If you're the kind of person who loves to act as a connector in your social life, take it a step further and plan a networking party. Traditional professional networking can be boring and awkward, but there are definitely ways to make it more fun and approachable.

### HOW IT WORKS

There are two ways to go about planning a networking event. The first involves inviting a bunch of friends and acquaintances over with the clear intention that everyone will be chatting about what they want in terms of professional growth. Attendees may be a mix of people in different industries, but that's okay—you never know where unexpected connections may be made. The second option is to plan more intimate dinners with all of your friends and acquaintances who work in similar industries, which can help facilitate more streamlined conversations.

## Learn about New (and Funny) Topics with a PowerPoint Salon

The words *fun* and *PowerPoint* are rarely ever used in the same sentence, but I swear after this event you'll consider them synonymous.

### HOW IT WORKS

Choose a small handful of your most outgoing, funny friends who are interested in being presenters; the rest of the partygoers can watch. Next, assign or have presenters pick out unexpected topics for their PowerPoint presentations. You can task them with making a niche history lesson funny, or they can even create satirical presentations on themselves, like "My Celebrity Crushes." Once everyone arrives, connect a laptop to your television or a wall projector and have everyone watch and ask questions about the presentations. Everyone will be busting up laughing by the end, wanting to present their own at the next one.

## Host a Book Swap

How many books currently sitting on your shelf have been collecting dust for the last year or longer, while you pine for new ones to crack open? If you just took a forlorn glance over at your stack, it's time to plan a book swap.

You and your friends can bring all your unwanted books together in the same place so people can grab the ones they want while the rest get donated to charity. If you're having a hard time parting with any of your books or want them back after your friends are done reading, try picking one book out of your collection for each of your participating friends. You'll hand out the books you've picked for one another with the knowledge that they were handpicked just for you. If five friends participated in the swap, you'll be heading home with five new books to read!

# CHAPTER 3

# Get Active

If you're not the kind of person who regularly wants to hit the gym, believe me, you're not alone. Fortunately, you can have a really good time using other ways to keep your body in motion. Getting used to incorporating more movement in your day takes time, but it helps when you're actually enjoying the stuff you're doing.

Getting active doesn't have to be something you do solo, either. It can actually be an awesome way to bond with friends, your kids, or your partner, and it may even give you reasons to get together more regularly.

If you're having a hard time picturing how you might incorporate physical fitness into your social life, don't worry, because that's what this whole chapter is about. From simple activities like meeting up with friends for morning walks to making all new friends by joining a recreational sports league, the possibilities are limitless.

## Greet the Day with Outdoor Yoga

Feeling in need of a little stretch? Invite friends over for some sun salutations in your backyard, on your patio, or on the rooftop. Ask them to bring their own mats, or, if you plan on making this a regular thing, grab a couple of inexpensive ones from your local Marshalls or T.J. Maxx and keep them stored in the corner of your entryway closet.

**BONUS TIP**

There are tons of easy online yoga programs to use if you don't want to lead the practice yourself, including free ones on *YouTube* like the über-popular Yoga with Adriene. Set out a couple of carafes of mint and lemon water to keep hydrated, and keep the zen mood going with some relaxing music.

## Get Bouncy with Friends at a Trampoline Class

Participating in a workout class with friends is a great way to keep accountable—once you sign up there's no backing out! The problem? Once you hop on your stationary bike or yoga mat, there isn't much socializing to do. Instead, try bouncing together at a trampoline class, where you can burn some major calories side by side while laughing it out. Studies have shown that a trampoline workout has a bevy of benefits: Not only does it strengthen the core, but it helps with balance, coordination, and even circulation. While you and your friends are having a great time bouncing around, your body's lymphatic system will also be stimulated, flushing toxins and helping to fight against disease. Win-win!

## Coordinate a Group Hike

Getting outside is even more fun when good friends and beautiful views are involved. Before making a plan, take a look at the forecast. Pick an upcoming weekend with the best-looking weather and consult your friends on social media to crowdsource the best hiking spots. Chances are you'll get tons of recommendations to keep in your back pocket for future outings. For now, pick the one that sounds the best and just go! You and your friends will have a great time taking in the fresh air. Make sure to bring sunscreen, plenty of water, and a few snacks to enjoy while out on the trail.

## Join an Intramural Sports League

Sporting leagues are a wonderful way to meet fun, active people in your area. And there are usually many options to choose from, whether you've wanted to give kickball a try or you prefer something less tiring like darts or billiards. Before signing up for one, it's important to think about what you'd like to get out of the experience. Are you a competitive person looking for some semi-serious sport, or someone who is mainly participating for the social activities? Answering that question will help determine which league, and which team, you'll want to join.

## Go for a Heart-Pumping Bike Ride Around Town

On the next sunny day, grab a group of your friends together for a bike ride around town. Getting around on a set of wheels instead of walking will allow you to check out more in a shorter amount of time, whether cruising by the water and stopping at the park or challenging yourselves to reach a new part of the city. If bike rides are something you want to incorporate into your life more regularly, start a morning bike group with routes that you designate before each ride. That way you can bike harder and faster, and you can make your two-wheeled meetups less about leisure and more about working out.

## Connect with Your Parent over a Round of Golf

Has one of your parents been hitting the green regularly for as long as you can remember? Surprise them with the ultimate gift: your presence. It will mean the world to them that you're showing an interest in their hobby, even if you have to fake it to start.

**BONUS TIP**

Start out with an afternoon at a driving range, where you can down a confidence beer and practice your swing before braving the wilds of the actual course. After that, make a date with your parent to head out for a morning tee time filled with bonding, laughs, and maybe another confidence beer.

## Meet Up in the Park for an Early-Morning Walk

Leisurely morning walks that culminate with sitting down with a friend at the café are a relaxing way to start any day, but if you're looking for something to raise your heart rate a little, try this more active version.

### HOW IT WORKS

Power walking is great exercise that may even be superior to running in multiple ways, especially if you want to add a social component. For most people, talking while running is out of the question, but you can definitely strike up a conversation while power walking. Not to mention that walking results in fewer injuries than running—the fewest injuries of any aerobic exercise, actually. It's also a much lower-impact exercise on your body, so you're less likely to suffer from any long-term physical effects as a result.

## Replace Happy Hour with an Hour of Sweat

Do you want to see your friends but without spending more money on drinks at a bar? Swap happy hour for an hour of activity, whether you decide on a boutique fitness class you've all been meaning to try, a workout in the park, or a power walk in a pretty area of your city. Your friends may be resistant to the idea at first, but they'll end up feeling good after swapping the empty booze calories for ones burned. The best part is that you all retain that time to catch up, and when you head home, the rest of your night isn't totally shot due to one too many margaritas.

## Skip the Mall and Shop Small Around Your Neighborhood

The next time you and your friends decide to indulge in a little retail therapy, ditch the mall. Instead, head over to the outdoor shopping district of your town, even if it means you'll have to walk from one neighborhood to the next in search of the best stores. Your group will get a lot more steps in with the added bonus of supporting local businesses. And the items you find will be more unusual than the ones you'd bring home from the big-name retailers.

### BONUS TIP

Seek out the thrift and vintage shops in your area during your next shopping trip. A big thrift store means more time on your feet digging around the racks for diamonds in the rough, and you may even come out with a major steal.

## Throw a Frisbee Around at the Park

There are tons of ways to get active with friends in the park, from classic activities like playing Frisbee and throwing a ball to new-wave group games like Spikeball, which is played by bouncing a ball off a small trampoline. Bring a bunch of different options so you don't have to choose until you arrive. Once you find an ideal spot, set up a few blankets in the grass picnic-style, but don't spend your whole afternoon lazing around on them. Try to challenge yourself to stay active and on your feet for at least half the time. Don't forget to bring water to regularly hydrate, too, especially if you're heading to the park in the summertime.

## Play Doubles Tennis

If you're a naturally competitive person, tennis may be the perfect recreational sport to try. It's fairly intuitive, making it easy to pick up with a good amount of practice. Once you get the hang of the basics, you can start playing doubles, which consists of teams of two on each side of the net. Grab your significant other or an equally competitive friend to be your doubles partner, and you'll have lots of fun kicking butt together. Challenge another couple or two of your friends to a game at your local park or sports club, where you can build your teamwork skills while breaking a sweat. It's also fun to play against strangers, who may end up becoming your friends if they aren't sore losers!

## Take Walking Meetings with Colleagues

Having one-on-one meetings in an office can feel so stiff. Next time, especially if the meeting is with one of your work buddies, take it outside the building for a walk around the block. For meetings that are at least thirty minutes long, you can also take the opportunity to grab a coffee down the street with your colleague. Your meeting may benefit from the lack of formality. The casual vibe lets you both be more at ease, allowing thoughts and ideas to flow more freely. Plus, putting in some extra steps in the afternoon always feels good.

**BONUS TIP**

Instead of having a sad desk salad for lunch tomorrow, schedule a solid amount of time to eat lunch outside with your colleagues. The fresh air and movement in your body as you walk to and from the park or another outdoor lunch spot helps prevent the dreaded afternoon slump.

## Try Slacklining (Anywhere!)

Slacklining is the kind of activity that requires a bit of practice, but the challenge makes it even more rewarding once you get it down. The great thing about slacklining is that you can do it anywhere that has anchor points to attach your line to. Whether you're hanging out at the park with friends or camping somewhere beautiful, any two trees or poles can serve as a spot for building your skill while getting active in the process.

### HOW IT WORKS

All you need to get started is a beginner's kit with a 2-inch-wide line and a ratchet system. Set the slackline close to the ground to eliminate any anxiety you might feel about falling off, and keep the line tight so that it doesn't sway or bounce as you walk across. Using a buddy as a balance aid as you gain your footing is also recommended, making it the perfect physical activity to do with friends!

## Make Game Night an Active One

While you probably enjoy a good game of Catan as much as the next person, sometimes it's more fun to have people over for an active game night. Charades, Twister, Wii Sports, and bowling are all fun, physically engaging activities that will have you and your friends on your feet rather than sitting on the couch the entire night. Another option is Ping-Pong, as well as bar games like darts and billiards. Those with backyards could also host an al fresco hangout, where you can play a fun game of soccer in between grilling and chilling.

## Try Partner Yoga

Often called "couples' yoga," partner yoga doesn't need to be performed by two people in a romantic relationship—it can also be practiced by friends! Partner yoga is a great way to build closeness and trust in any relationship, bringing people together through movement, breath, and form. If you feel a strong bond with a friend, or have a significant other who is also interested in yoga, ask if they would be interested in practicing partner yoga with you; there are a countless number of poses you can learn together. The foundation of partner yoga is using one another to stretch deeper into certain poses. Some focus mainly on breath work, so you can try it even if you aren't an advanced yogi.

## Cool Down with Water Sports

Whether the closest body of water to you is a lake, river, or ocean, you can indulge in a number of activities to get your adrenaline racing. Enjoy stand-up paddleboarding (SUP), kayaking, and swimming in any body of water. On a lake, you and your friends can wakeboard and water ski, and the ocean provides opportunities for surfing and riding vehicles like Jet Skis and Sea-Doos. Next time you find yourself on the river, try an activity like fishing, canoeing, or even rafting the rapids if you're feeling daring.

## Coordinate a Workout Class for the Whole Office

If you're feeling lethargic after work, chances are your colleagues might be feeling the same way. To help kick everyone out of their postwork funk, try scheduling a workout class for the entire office to participate in.

### HOW IT WORKS

Many fitness studios are available for buyouts, from spinning to HIIT classes. If you're able to expense the workout, that means a free class, and if not, you'll most likely be able to negotiate a lower group rate directly through the studio. Another option is bringing an instructor into your office to lead a group stretching, yoga, or meditation class. If one of your colleagues is already an accredited instructor and interested in leading regular afternoon sessions, even better!

## Work Your Arms at an Indoor Rock-Climbing Gym

File this one under major workouts that don't actually feel like a workout. Indoor rock-climbing gyms usually provide two different kinds of climbing walls: the traditional, tall obstacle course, which you climb while wearing a harness, and freestyle bouldering. If you've never been to a climbing gym before, start on the normal rock wall to get a feel for how to find the right handholds and footholds. Once you've got the hang of climbing, the bouldering wall presents a real challenge. In bouldering, climbers aren't attached with straps, so you'll rely on the strength of your arms, legs, and core to keep yourself moving upward. This is the kind of activity you'll want to bring a friend along for, too, both because it'll be more fun together and so that you can act as spotters for each other.

## Have Friends over for a Dance Party

Breaking into spontaneous dance in your own living room is one of the most fun ways to get sweaty, so how about doing it with a whole group of friends? Getting started is simple: Clear space in the largest part of your home to maximize mobility potential, then turn on an energetic playlist that you know will keep people on their feet and moving.

**BONUS TIP**

Before the party, ask your friends if they have any favorite throwback songs to add to the playlist, or make it collaborative by using a platform like Spotify. If you feel like challenging yourselves, try searching on websites like *YouTube* for dance routines to your favorite songs to learn together.

## Reconnect on FaceTime While Walking

It can be difficult to find the time to call long-distance friends and family members. The longer you go between catch-ups, the more daunting they can feel when you know how much ground there is to cover. Instead of sitting on your sofa or bed when you finally get around to dialing them, try going for a walk around your neighborhood as you chat, showing them your favorite local sights and homes in your area on FaceTime. You'll complete the catch-up while also getting your steps in for the day—win-win!

## Roller-Skate Around Town

A great activity to do with friends, family, or a romantic partner, getting around on roller skates is not only a fun and nostalgic means of transportation—it's a workout! If you haven't skated in a while, get back into it the safe way with a night at a roller rink, where you can practice without much fear of getting hurt. Roller-skating rinks are also a fun place to spend time in their own right. Once you've gotten your sea legs back under you, try skating around the park and with a partner. Reward yourselves with a little ice cream before you head back home.

## Set Up Regular Running Dates

When you set a fitness goal to start running on a regular basis, one of the best ways to stay accountable is to bring a friend or partner along with you. Together, you'll be able to track your routes and your progress as you set new goals every time you hit the pavement. Set up a weekly run date with a friend who you know won't bail on you, and challenge one another to continually crush your personal bests. Before you get started, download a mobile application that will track your progress and your routes. You can also find a handy cardio app to have on hand in case you want to try some burpees in the park afterward.

## Tackle a Bike-and-Brew Trail

A bike-and-brew trail is typically a scenic route for bikers to take, marked at intervals with craft breweries for hanging out with fellow bikers and enjoying a cold one. These kinds of trails aren't only for experienced bikers, though. Just make sure to choose a route without a steep incline or challenging terrain and you're set.

### HOW IT WORKS

Next time the weather is agreeable, bring a friend and map out how far you two want to bike. Find markers on the way of places to take a break to enjoy the view or a sip of water, and breweries where you can stop for a refreshing glass or flight. Make sure not to overdo it, and to always bike responsibly. If there aren't any ale trails in your area, a scenic bike ride that ends with a beer back in town works just as well.

## Have a Deep-Cleaning Exercise Day

Let a session of deep cleaning act as your workout for the day. It'll feel great to hit two birds with one stone, spending an afternoon getting your place guest-ready by scrubbing out all the dust and grime. This activity feels satisfying to complete, and at the same time you'll move around and burn calories for hours without even noticing it. When you reframe cleaning as exercise, chores like dishwashing and vacuuming become arm workouts, and moving furniture or heavier items around to redecorate engage your core. Make it even more fun with a pumped-up playlist to keep you moving, and don't be afraid to take dance breaks.

## Play Around at the Beach or Lake

Some people like to head to the waterfront to relax and tan for hours, and there's absolutely nothing wrong with that. The key is to recruit a good mix of active and passive beach-goers on your next trip so that you can experience the best of both worlds in one afternoon. Lying on the sand is always fun, but you can also break up the afternoon with bouts of activity: swimming, playing catch, going for a run along the shore. It'll make lying back down and enjoying a cold beverage feel even better—guaranteed.

## Take the Stairs

If you're ready to kick your glutes into high gear, try a month of swearing off the elevator unless absolutely necessary. To help you in your quest, create a challenge by asking one friend to do the same, and tell them to choose one person to ask, and so on. Pretty soon you and all your friends will be running up and down steps all over town working on your summer bods. It's always easier to keep challenging yourself if your friends are focused on the same goal—especially when it's literally kicking your butt.

## Plan Fun Family Outings

If you inspire your kids to love physical activity, they'll benefit from it for life. It's a two-way street, too, as the more active you inspire your kids to be, the more you'll want to be active yourself. Start by planning some fun activities to do together as a family—pretty much anything that revolves around spending time outside and not playing video games or lying around looking at their phones is good. Try simple things you can do in a couple of hours, like heading to the park to play tag and catch. On the weekend, head over to hiking trails, botanical gardens, and the river or lake for something that will keep them (and you) screen-free for the entire day.

## Reconnect with Your Favorite Childhood Sport

While you were growing up, you were probably obsessed with a certain sport. You spent your time after school every day practicing with your teammates, and you played games on the weekends. At some point, many of us grow up and move on from playing team sports, but that doesn't mean you've lost your love for it. Intramural teams are a no-brainer option, but they can require a large time commitment. For certain sports like tennis, soccer, and basketball, check out recreational sport groups on sites like *Meetup* and *Facebook*, or try heading to your local park and playing a game of pickup with whoever is there. Once you've made those connections and know generally when these groups play, it'll be easy for you to join them.

## Take a Dance Cardio Class

If gyms aren't really your thing, but you're still looking for a way to get active, try a dance fitness class. You'll get just as good a cardio workout without all the boring burpees and classic push-ups. Plus, dancing releases happy chemicals like oxytocin in your brain, and listening to joyful music serves you a hit of dopamine. Add that to the serotonin you get from the sense of connectedness you'll feel being around others and the endorphins triggered by your body moving and sweating, and you've got a veritable happiness cocktail! There are also dance cardio classes for participants of every skill level, so you can start anywhere you feel comfortable and work your way up to more complicated routines.

## Set Exercise Goals with Your Partner

If you're in a relationship, treat your partner like a built-in workout buddy. Together, you can help each other hit your personal goals and stay motivated. Research has shown that working out with your significant other can build serious bonds, and relationship counselors often encourage couples to exercise together, as it helps you to hold each other accountable.

### HOW IT WORKS

There's no one right way to plan and execute fitness goals with your partner, but one of the easiest is to make your workouts into challenges. Whoever can do the most squats gets dinner cooked for them that night, or whoever works out the most nights in a row gets to pick the next movie. You can also integrate fun, physical activities into your weekend dates, going for bike rides together, hiking, or trying a nouveau fitness class.

## Get Into Gardening

Believe it or not, developing a green thumb does way more for you than just help you create an amazing-looking garden. You'll spend more time outside, and yard work definitely qualifies as exercise, so it's the perfect way to spend an afternoon when you aren't planning on hitting the gym or going for a run. Gardening can also be a family activity, and tasks can get done quickly when everyone is using top-notch teamwork skills. Alternate what each family member works on; one day you and your partner can work on planting or pruning while your kids mow the lawn. Next time you go to the garden, switch tasks.

## Become a Part-Time Dog Walker

Whether you're in the market for a casual side hustle or simply looking to spend more time with fluffy friends, walking dogs for a few hours each week is a fun way to schedule some extra physical activity. Start by asking any of your dog-owning friends if they need regular help with dog walking, and check out websites like *Rover* and *Wag!*, which make it easy to create a dog-walking profile that allows you to connect with dog owners in your area.

Another option is to post your availability on social media or on a neighborhood forum app like Nextdoor. You'll probably meet quite a few new friends while out on your walks, too, as people come over for a chance to pet the dogs.

# CHAPTER 4

# Plan a More Creative Date Night

When was the last time you and your partner tried out a date night activity other than sitting down for dinner at a restaurant? If you're having a hard time answering that question, it's okay! It's easy to get caught in a romance rut, defaulting to dinner and a movie, especially if you two have been together for a long time. But it's never too late to plan a more creative date night—or day—or weekend! All you need is a little inspiration.

This chapter is all about providing you with silly, creative, romantic ideas to help spice up your time with your special person. Besides the obvious benefit of having more fun together, trying new things as a couple can lead to long-term relationship health. Research has shown that sharing adventures helps people be vulnerable with their partner, inviting growth and maturity into your relationship.

Why not try something new this weekend, like skipping dinner altogether and heading straight for dessert, cozying up at a drive-in theater, or planning a spontaneous staycation? These are just some of the ways you two can choose to step outside of the date night box. The next move is yours!

## Learn a New Skill Together

It's time to ditch the typical dinner date. Research suggests that working together to learn new skills can strengthen your bond with your partner, and there are many ways to make learning together super fun. Whether you've been dying to try a sushi-making course, or your partner has always had an interest in pottery, watching each other discover a new passion can reignite some sparks (and maybe some laughter along the way).

If it's a skill neither of you have tried before, start by signing up for a one-time intro-level class to gauge whether or not you both enjoy it before diving in all the way. If it doesn't end up being your thing, that's okay! Just try the next one on your list. Otherwise, ask your instructor about long-term courses, which will give you regular opportunities to connect and learn together.

## Challenge Each Other to Games at a Dive Bar

Date night doesn't have to always be fancy. Instead, head over to your local dive for a night of billiards and darts. Most bars that have pool tables function on a coin-operated system, so stock up on quarters. When you get there, take turns challenging each other in one-on-one games. After each game ends, head to the bar, where the loser buys the next round. It's fun to see your partner's competitive side come out, but try keeping things a little playful too. One good way to do that is to bring another couple to play with as teams, or meet new friends at the bar by challenging them to a game. That way, you'll also get to call upon your teamwork skills.

## Plan a Romantic Staycation

Did a new hotel just open up in your city? Check it out together with an overnight stay, which can be just as romantic as heading out of town for the weekend. An added bonus: You don't have to worry about forgetting to pack something, since you can easily go grab it, and you'll spend virtually no money on gas. For a full evening of staycation bliss, have dinner at the hotel restaurant, then hit the bar for a nightcap, or bring your own bottle of wine to enjoy in the room.

## Take a Brewery or Distillery Tour

Have you ever wondered how your favorite beer or spirit is made? Brewery and distillery tours are a fun, interactive way of learning something new together (and sometimes they include tastings too!). Usually available to book directly through the distillery, the tour will take you on a quick jaunt behind the scenes to see how pure ingredients like agave, corn, rye, or hops are mashed and dis-tilled into the favorite bottle now sit-ting in your liquor cabinet. After you're done with the tour, don't miss cozying up at the bar together to continue the tasting on your own.

## Build a Bucket List

Ready to see the world but not sure where to start? Have a romantic night in together, working your way through a bottle of wine while you discuss your own personal bucket lists and see where they intersect. You'll learn more about each other by listening to your partner explain (and make a case for) their ultimate life must-dos. At the end of the night, you'll have a master list that you created together, detailing how you plan on tackling the fun stuff.

**BONUS TIP**

Build your shared bucket list to be as diverse as possible, mixing in more extravagant items like visiting the Taj Mahal with more approachable ones, like taking a hot-air balloon ride or seeing your favorite artist in concert. That way, you're more likely to start ticking items off your list right away, rather than watching the list collect dust.

## Cozy Up at a Drive-In Theater

Movie nights at home can be cute, but sometimes you need to get out of the house. A drive-in movie is a great, balanced option for when you don't want to be sitting on your couch anymore, but you also don't feel like being social with anyone else. Seeing a movie at the drive-in also means you aren't stuck in an uncomfortable seat, and you won't have to be completely silent the whole time. Instead, you and your partner get to hop in your car with snacks, blankets, pillows, and comfy clothes—all the best ingredients for watching a show. Choose a flick that will make you want to get even cozier with your partner, like a scary movie or a romantic comedy.

## Get Artsy at a Gallery or Museum Event

You and your partner may not be art critics, but you could become a pair of them for a night out at a museum or gallery event. If you're both members of a local art museum, first check their website for weekend events. Many museums and galleries plan evenings when the exhibits stay open late, and sometimes the artists even make an appearance to help draw interest. Another place to find upcoming events is to subscribe to the newsletter for your favorite museum or gallery, so you'll be the first to hear when new programming is announced. Bonus points if you find one that provides guests with finger foods and beverages, and museum members should keep their eye out for annual benefits and galas that give you and your S.O. a chance to dress up for a special night.

## Go Dancing—Just the Two of You

Going dancing with friends is fun for obvious reasons, but going with just your partner is a different experience altogether. Hitting the dance floor with pals is a lighthearted way to get your body moving to some of your favorite songs, while choosing dancing for your date night can be much more sensual. Dance dates can take on so many different vibes as well. Some nights the two of you may want to groove to Latin music; other nights you may want to shake it to hip-hop. If you don't feel comfortable getting out there yet, try taking a dance class together first.

## Enlist a Professional Picnic Service

Take advantage of whatever natural surroundings you have in your area—a sprawling park, a beach, picturesque meadows—and hire a service to set up a fancy picnic for you. While you could always arrange a picnic yourself, leaving the setup to professionals has its advantages. The main one is that you can just focus on having a fun, romantic time with your partner, arriving at the location together and feeling that initial moment of surprise and delight, and not having to worry about cleaning up.

Booking your picnic through a service also means that they are already clued in to the little details it takes to make your picnic feel luxe and special, like providing napkins, a trash can, and a cooler of spa water and champagne on ice. Sometimes you've got to treat yourself!

## Wind Down with Candlelit Yoga

After a stressful workweek, there's nothing more centering than a night of treating your minds and bodies to a calming session of candlelit yoga. It's an activity you can facilitate privately in your own living room, or one that you can seek out at a local studio. Without the bright lights, you and your partner will feel more relaxed and less self-conscious about how flexible you are or how well you're hitting each pose. After your session is over, keep up the relaxation theme for the rest of the night, taking a hot shower together and simply watching your favorite show or movie before tucking in early.

## Wake Up Early and Get Breakfast Together

Dates don't have to take place in the evening. While it can be easy to fall into a routine of hitting the snooze button for as long as possible, that can lead to a lot of stress, as the two of you are forced to rush out of the house to avoid being late to work.

But if you both make a commitment to wake up a bit earlier—even just one day a week—you'll give yourselves precious, uninterrupted time to spend together in the morning. Factoring in enough time to get out of the house together before work begins is even better, offering opportunities to take peaceful walks, grab a lazy breakfast, or check out a nearby coffee shop together before having to think about work for the day.

## Upgrade Your Home Bar

This weekend, bring the bar home with you. Having all the ingredients for creating delicious cocktails and mocktails makes staying in together even more fun, as you get creative playing bartender for each other.

**HOW IT WORKS**

Start by picking out a fun recipe book together, zeroing in on a certain cocktail style you both enjoy. Maybe tiki drinks float your boats, or you love the idea of Prohibition-era cocktails. Next, pick a few that look the most enticing, with one easier-to-make option and one or two more challenging concoctions. Hit up your local grocer and liquor market together and then get to shaking and stirring at home! Once you feel confident in your skill, invite friends over—they're sure to be impressed. If you're not big drinkers, there are tons of zero-ABV liquor options now that taste just as good as the original, if not better.

## Have a Hands-On Dining Experience

Bond with each other by taking a fun, hands-on approach to dining—bonus points if it's a cuisine one or neither of you has tried before. Chinese hot pot, Korean barbecue, or Swiss fondue are all great options. If you're both big food lovers, you'll have even more fun together at dinner when you get to play around with flavor combinations yourselves. As long as you both keep an open mind, it's a win-win as you learn more about a new culture through its culinary offerings and show each other that you're not afraid to step outside of your own gastronomic comfort zone.

**BONUS TIP**

If your partner ends up obsessing over how fun it was to make your own waffles or drip oozy cheese on bread, you now have a great option for their next birthday or holiday gift.

## Rent a Fancy Car for the Weekend

There's something so timeless and romantic about the idea of cruising down a scenic highway in the seats of a fancy car, especially when you can drop the top. Whether you and your partner dream about zipping along in a modern sports car or throwing it back with a vintage convertible, renting a special ride for a weekend can provide you with the perfect excuse to go on some fun day trips, making a full afternoon out of driving out to the lake or simply winding your way through rolling pastoral hills. For extra drama, get all dressed up for the occasion, including a silky headscarf and your favorite sunglasses.

## Take a Romantic Bath Together

Hopping into the tub together for a long bath is such a simple, relaxing way to connect with your person. Stop by the closest bath and body store and make an activity of it, sniffing your way through their enormous selection of colorful bath bombs that can do anything from turning the water in your tub into a rainbow to making it smell like the ocean. Some shops even have a "make your own" station for bath bombs and salts, where you can work together to pick out your own custom fragrance.

When you get home, set up some romantic mood lighting in the form of candles (be careful where you place them, though!), pop open a bottle of wine or shake up some refreshing mocktails, and get ready to bond.

## Swap Small Gifts

Have you and your partner figured out what your individual love languages are? Your love language determines the dominant method by which you prefer to give and receive love, whether through acts of kindness, physical touch, quality time, words of affirmation, or gift giving. If you or your partner is the latter type, honor that with an evening of exchanging small gifts you purchased for one another.

Just make sure you don't shop for the gifts together! Choose a separate time to head to the store alone and pick up whatever you think your partner would delight in receiving: a new pair of unique socks, a scented candle, a new tool for their kit, a cute toy for your pet, a bouquet of fresh flowers. Exchange them after dinner when you're relaxing, and then take time to show your appreciation.

## Laugh Together at a Comedy Show

Life is too short to take ourselves too seriously, which is why laughing with your partner is one of the best ways to connect. Make your next date night one to remember by checking out your city's comedy offerings, whether it be famous traveling comedians, smaller up-and-coming acts, or improvisation showcases. Regardless of what you two land on, go into the experience with an open mind, ready to create some funny memories together. Something to keep in mind: The closer you sit to the front, the more likely it will be that the comedian or improv artist will try to interact with you or pull you onstage!

## Reconnect with Old Friends Through Double Dating

Keeping up with a demanding job. Making time for romance in your relationship. Staying on top of...well, life! Sometimes it's tough to schedule time with friends when other aspects of every-day life keep getting in the way. Setting up double dates is an easy way to connect with old friends while not neglecting your partner, and you can make new friends, too, either with a colleague you're just getting to know or through your partner's circle. Pick a fun activity, like bowling or trivia night, that will have you all laughing and interacting in new ways, rather than just sitting across from each other at dinner.

## Re-create Your First Date

Re-creating your first date can be a playful way of reigniting the initial spark in your relationship. Whether you first decided to meet up at a cocktail bar in your old neighborhood or at the rustic Italian spot across town, return to that place and reminisce on all the great times you two have shared together since that fateful day. For extra fun, arrive separately and pretend like you just met. You can ask each other cheeky questions that you may think you already know the answer to, but who knows? Your partner could surprise you.

**BONUS TIP**

If you don't plan on feigning your first meeting, let your server know that you two have returned for nostalgic reasons. Chances are you'll make their day, and they may just give you guys an extra cocktail or slice of cake.

## Skip Dinner and Go Straight for Dessert

Who made the rule that you have to eat your dinner before your dessert? On your next date night, skip the formality of a sit-down dinner and head straight to a dessert bar to share a sweet treat or two and chat the night away. Most dessert bars also offer drinks, so you can pair your chocolate gâteau with an espresso martini, or your lemon meringue pie with a vodka smash. If you don't have a dessert bar where you live, a milkshake at your local diner works just as well, and you can order fries to dip (don't knock it until you try it).

## Wander Around IKEA

Not just a quirky activity from the movie *(500) Days of Summer*, taking a leisurely trip through IKEA is a really fun thing to do with your partner. At IKEA, an affordable Swedish home and furniture retailer, the store is an enormous maze of staged rooms where you follow a laid-out path. First, stop by the food court to fuel up on Swedish meatballs with gravy and lingonberry sauce. Next, take to the winding aisles, comparing your favorite rooms and picking up practical tchotchkes along the way for your kitchen and living room. If you don't live together yet, this activity may help you picture what it would be like to shop for a shared home.

**BONUS TIP**

If you don't live near an IKEA, no problem! Instead, pick a few local interior design and antique shops to explore as well as a lunch spot where you can refuel between stops.

## Try Something Daring Together

Channel your inner adrenaline junkie—and impress your partner—by picking an activity that will raise both of your heart rates. While most nights might be spent relaxing on the sofa (which can be fun too), seeking adventure together is an essential way to grow and maintain your bond. Skydiving, speed racing, and off-roading are all daring date activities that will push you to your limits and hopefully bring you two even closer. But the word *daring* means something different to every couple, so make sure to discuss this with your partner before setting up that scuba diving lesson.

## Set Up a Blind Taste Test

They say that when one of your five senses is diminished, your other four are heightened. Try the theory out for yourselves with a blind taste test. One partner will be doing the cooking and the other the tasting. If you're the one preparing the food, blindfold your partner while you put together bites of food for them. Have them try each one and guess what it is. Make sure to provide a variety of flavors and textures, juxtaposing cold bites like salami and smoked salmon with warmer ones, and don't forget to have them take sips of different drinks in between. It's an activity that will be fun for both of you. Next time it'll be your turn to play the taste tester.

## Try Out a Paint-and-Sip

Have you ever seen your partner try something creative? Or vice versa? Let your artistic side shine through for once with a paint-and-sip class. This is an especially great activity if you both have day jobs that don't usually allow you to tap in to your creativity.

### HOW IT WORKS

To ensure a successful paint-and-sip date, go in with an open mind, ready to push yourselves out of your comfort zones, be silly, and learn something new. When you arrive, you'll be given a small canvas, brushes, and glasses for wine. Some paint-and-sip classes choose one classic work of art for everyone to attempt to re-create, but others allow you to paint whatever you want. Who knows if you'll want to hang your masterpieces after all is said and done, but it'll be a fun time regardless.

## Spend the Afternoon at a Day Spa

Couples' massages can be awkward, but you don't need to book a treatment to have a good time together at a day spa. Instead, check for one in your area that charges a flat fee for entry and offers a variety of different areas for at-leisure relaxation, like pools, hot tubs, saunas, and steam rooms. You and your partner can spend a whole afternoon hopping around from one station to the next, sipping on spa water and feeling pampered as a couple. For an extra dose of TLC, try bringing two hydrating sheet masks that you can use in the steam room—you'll leave with baby-soft skin.

## Indulge In Couples' Retail Therapy

At the turn of the season, when you're both in need of a few new closet staples, take a trip to your favorite shopping area together. You'll be able to provide a second opinion for each other, and will have the opportunity to hear how good you look in those new jeans and say how much that new jacket suits them. For even more fun, take turns picking out pieces for each other to try on, or, if you really trust your partner's style decisions, try splitting up to buy a surprise piece for each other.

**BONUS TIP**

If the two of you shop at different stores, make an effort to not rush your partner as they take their time in their favorite shop. Be encouraging, even if what they're trying on isn't your style—it's all about how confident they feel in the outfit that matters.

## Go for a Hike at Dawn or Dusk

Heading out on a popular hike in the middle of the day on a week-end ensures you'll have no privacy. For a romantic hiking date, it's nice to feel that magical sense that you're the only two people in the world, allowing you to indulge in some PDA. Avoid the crowds by hiking up to a gorgeous vantage point right before dawn or at the golden hour before sunset. It may be tough to wake up before dawn for a strenuous activity, but when you two are alone, experiencing the sunrise, it'll be worth it.

**BONUS TIP**

To make your sunrise moment feel even better, pack a thermos of hot coffee and some granola bars or pastries to enjoy together at the peak. You'll avoid feeling sluggish on your way back.

## Make Breakfast for Dinner

Don't know what to make for dinner tonight? One of the fun things about being an adult is that you can choose to eat whatever you want—so why not make pancakes, bacon, and eggs for dinner? Or, if you don't even feel like cooking, take a trip over to a late-night neighborhood diner for some greasy spoon breakfast favorites and a round of milkshakes to boot. If you do choose to make your breakfast-dinner at home, really lean in to the Sunday morning vibe by wearing your coziest pajamas and turning on some nostalgic cartoons to watch together while you devour your meal.

## Cook a Fancy Candlelit Dinner Together

A night out at a romantic restaurant is always fun, but it can set you back a pretty penny. Instead, try putting your heads together to come up with a delicious meal to make all on your own. You'll get total control of what goes into the meal (hello, butter lovers and extra-cheese fiends) and will get to enjoy all of the fanciness without any of the potential stuffiness.

**HOW IT WORKS**

To get started, scour the Internet for fun recipes that look tasty but approachable, then hit your local grocer to grab the ingredients. Depending on who is the better cook, one of you can act as the sous chef, taking on tasks like cutting vegetables and draining pasta, while the other handles the rest. Bon appétit!

## Attend a Niche Trivia Night

Are you and your partner Lord of the Rings fans? Potterheads? Medieval history buffs? If so, your chance to be rewarded for your extremely niche shared knowledge has finally arrived by way of a local trivia night. No matter where you live, you're bound to find lots of bars in town that offer trivia nights every week, if not more often. Many of them stick to general trivia, but some switch up the theme every week and would likely be open to suggestions. Now all you have to do is come up with your team name.

## Glide Around a Skating Rink

A classic date night activity, skating is a fun way to cap off your evening together. During wintertime, outdoor ice-skating rinks are super romantic, and warmer months lend themselves to roller skating, though it can be done at an indoor rink at any time of the year. As you hit the rink and try to get reacquainted with the weird feeling of having wheels on your feet, you'll get to hang on to each other for support and act like kids all over again. For the ultimate night of nostalgia, stop for an ice cream cone after.

## Gaze Up at the Stars

What's more romantic than stargazing? The answer is nothing, especially when you and your partner drive away from your town or city to experience the full splendor of the night sky. Depending on where you live, check online to see if you're near an area that is designated a Dark Sky Place—internationally recognized destinations for the best stargazing anywhere. Download an app to help you spot constellations and learn more about their ancient backstories. If you plan to make a trip of it, bring sleeping bags, blankets, pillows, and snacks, and try overnight car camping.

## Hit the Arcade

If you and your partner aren't afraid of a little healthy competition, try heading to date night at the arcade. Chains like Dave & Buster's have locations nationwide and are marketed specifically at adults. There you can play classic fighting games, race each other in virtual cars and speedboats, or see who can make the most baskets in the shortest amount of time. Some arcades take it a step further and offer fun activities like cosmic golf, rock-climbing walls, and bocce ball. To make things interesting, wager the next dinner bill. Whoever loses the next game of Skee-Ball or dies first in *The House of the Dead* picks up the check.

## Go Treasure Hunting at Estate Sales

Take your vintage obsession to a new level by attending estate sales, where you can pick up killer deals together and have a great time poking around at all the unique objects you'll find. Come well prepared with cash in hand, a negotiating mindset, and a list of stuff you both are hoping to score. Regardless of what you end up taking home, the experience will be like a unique scavenger hunt as you check out clothing from bygone eras or spot amazingly crafted pieces of furniture for a fraction of the price that you might see at a big-name retailer.

## Tackle a Fun Home Project

Home projects can be tedious, but on date night pick something fun to work on together that will let you get creative and make your home feel even better to live in.

### HOW IT WORKS

First, discuss exactly what it is that you'll be working on together, whether it's adding a fun accent wall to your bedroom, setting up a cozy home theater, or building something that's totally DIY. Order the supplies for your project in advance or figure out where exactly you can pick it all up on the day of your date. Once it comes time to take action, try to be patient with one another and keep in mind that you're working as a team. By the end, you'll have strengthened your communication skills, and your place will get a nice little facelift.

## Plan a Romantic Scavenger Hunt

Perfect for a special occasion like an anniversary, birthday, or even a marriage proposal, scavenger hunts can take place anywhere, from as small an area as your home to around an entire city. First, decide on how wide you want that range to be, then pick your clues. If you'd like your partner to travel all around town for the hunt, choose a few different meaningful locations to plant your romantic clues, with personal hints that only your partner would know. Finally, you'll meet them at the end of the scavenger hunt with a gift or surprise. This amount of thoughtfulness and effort is sure to impress any partner.

# CHAPTER 5

# Reconnect
## with Your Family

As much as our families can drive us up a wall, we still love them at the end of the day. Every family, and the things they have been through together, is totally unique. Your family members know things about you that nobody else on earth does—like that one secret your sibling kept for you when you were kids.

Sometimes the fact that family is always there makes us take them for granted. That's totally normal and natural, and relationships between people (blood-related or not) can drift over time—especially if you and your family live in different parts of the world.

If you have been missing those bonding moments with your family members, this chapter is here to give you some easy tips on how to reinstate them—one fun activity and thought-ful gesture at a time. Some of them are silly, like re-enacting a childhood photo as adults, and some of them are more useful, like helping to decorate for the holidays. Because every person's situation is beautifully unique, feel free to use these tips to strengthen the bonds with your chosen family instead.

## Book a Weekend Together at an Airbnb

Spending family time at home is fun, but sometimes it helps to step out of that familiarity and into a new location where you can all bond even more. Regardless of whether the property is in the next town over or across the country, look for a place with ample space in the living room for playing games, and a feature you might not have at home but have always wanted, like a swimming pool or a billiards table. You'll have tons of fun relaxing and playing together in a space that feels fresh, without piled-up dishes or burdensome memories.

## Re-create Old Photos

Have siblings or cousins in town that you don't get to see very often? Next time you're reunited, take a walk down memory lane together, sifting through boxes and albums full of old family photos. Pick your favorites and have fun trying to re-create them as adults, copying the poses you did way back when and the clothing you wore as kids. You're guaranteed to share some good laughs together, and the old and new photos will serve as the perfect gag gift to send to family this holiday season. Looking through all those old photographs together will also bring up many opportunities for reminiscing together.

## Go See a Ball Game

Whether you're the kind of person who closely watches every play, or you're just there for the hot dogs and beer, a night of cheering on your local baseball team together is a great way to bond. The less sporty family members can learn a thing or two from the true fans, and you'll all have fun cheering together and absorbing the infectious energy of the crowd. Don't worry about getting prime seats, either! The main objective is to bond with your family members, and the energy at the back of the stadium is always the most fun anyway.

## Have a Phone-Free Period

This one might seem like a no-brainer, but keeping your eyes off your smartphone screen for an extended period of time is often easier said than done. Next time you and your sibs are together, or your whole family is having dinner, challenge yourselves to put your phones away for the entire evening to focus on having real conversations with one another. To make things easier, try throwing all your phones into a drawer or leaving them in a bowl by the door—out of sight, out of mind. You'll be surprised at how much easier it is to connect with one another when you're not all scrolling through *Instagram*.

## Put Together a Collection of Family Recipes

Create a lasting keepsake that you and your family will enjoy for generations in the form of a family cookbook. One of your parents may even have their own rough version of one already, written on notecards or scribbled into a notebook.

### HOW IT WORKS

Ask your immediate and extended family about any special recipes that they might want to contribute. After you've collected all the recipes for your book, you have a few options. You could ask the kids in your family to illustrate a few of your family's favorites, keep the collection simple and sleek, or even send it off to a freelance graphic designer to turn it into a masterpiece. Give the finished copies away at the next big holiday as your special gift.

## Get Tattoos Together

It may be easier convincing some members of your family than others that matching tattoos are a good idea, but if you can, do it! No matter what paths you and the members of your family take, or whether you end up relocating, you'll always have a little piece of them with you. And the most fun is the brainstorming phase, when you decide together which tattoo to get and where you'll put it. Have a family crest, a special quote you all love, or a symbol that reflects your culture? Those are good ideas to start with. For those who are more tattoo-averse, remind them that they can put it anywhere they want, like in a spot that is easily covered up by an article of clothing.

## Have a Backyard Barbecue

Backyard barbecues are an easy, relaxed way to get some quality family bonding time in. Whether your family is satisfied with classic hot dogs and hamburgers or you're looking to elevate things a bit, the key is spending an afternoon outside in one another's company. Don't have a backyard? Seek out a nearby park where you can grill, or simply stop by your favorite neighborhood grocer for grab-and-go dishes that make cleaning up a breeze. This is also the perfect time to try out the no-phones rule! Just make sure to bring plenty of activities to keep everyone entertained, like a soccer ball to kick around, a deck of cards, or water guns for the kids (and adults).

## Hit a Flea Market

The best flea market experiences happen when you have no expectations going in, allowing you and your family to have fun just perusing the stalls for unexpected treasures. Whether you find your favorite new vintage piece, a present to bring home to your grandparents, or scented candles for your mom's place, it'll be an adventure comparing quirky finds and getting inspired together by the one-of-a-kind wares. If you can't find a flea market in your area, garage sales work just as well, and you may be able to score even better deals if you bring your top bargaining skills.

## Start a Family Podcast Club

You can do this activity regardless of where your family members are in the world or how busy each one of you might be, since podcasts can be listened to while in transit or at your desk. Those of you located in the same area will now have a good reason to get together at least once per month, and those farther away can join in by video call. Alternate between podcasts that are just for fun and ones that help you bond more as a family, whether they include practical advice for snuffing out feuds and mending broken bonds, or have a plot that is centered around another (real or fictional) family.

## Help Your Parents Freshen Up Their Home for the Holidays

Offering to tweak the interior design of your parents' home could end up becoming a practice in patience, but a positive outcome is well worth the effort. Decorating for the upcoming holiday, whatever it might be, will help breathe new life into their space, and make hosting more enjoyable for them (and you) once the holidays roll around. It may also bring back nostalgic memories of doing so when you were younger.

## Surprise Your Sibling with a Babysitting Night

Next time you have a free night, rack up some major karma points by treating your sibling to a night of freedom. You'll get to bond more with your niece or nephew, and your sib will never forget your random act of kindness. Start by nonchalantly checking in to make sure they don't already have any big plans that night, then let them know that morning or the day before that you plan on coming over to look after their kid(s). That will hopefully give them enough time to plan their ideal escape without ruining the element of surprise.

**BONUS TIP**

If you want to take your act of kindness to the next level, plan something for them as a part of the surprise. Easy options include making dinner reservations, grabbing tickets to that movie they've been wanting to see, or booking them a much-needed massage.

## Dig Into Your Ancestry

Get the family together to learn more about the history of your ancestors, which can be an eye-opening and educational bonding experience for everyone. The senior members of your family will love sharing any stories of their parents' and grandparents' lives, which you'll be able to pass on to your own grandchildren someday.

### HOW IT WORKS

If you don't know where to start, try asking your grandparents for any names and information they have regarding known ancestors within your lineage. They'll most likely be happy you asked and will gladly offer up information if they have it. Using those clues, dig into public records available online, or visit a website like *Ancestry* that can do some of the sleuthing for you.

## Have a Throwback Movie Night

Nearly every family has a few favorite movies—the ones you used to watch over and over as kids. Next time you all get together, have a big movie night in your comfiest pajamas. Grab the kind of snacks you might have delighted in while growing up, like popcorn and your favorite candies and soda, and settle on the couch or set up blankets and pillows on the floor for the ultimate throwback experience. Take turns picking your favorite, most formative movies to watch together as you reminisce. If your family members are having a hard time deciding, write down a few options on pieces of paper and choose one from a hat. Take turns picking out one to watch.

## Start a New Family Tradition

Sometimes there's a good reason why you and your family members need to start a new tradition. Regardless of the "why," focus on how you want it to feel, and play around with different options. For example, head out as a unit to fun places like the aquarium or the amusement park, resolve to have a big pasta dinner every first Tuesday of the month, or agree to send each other postcards every time one of you travels to an exciting destination. New family traditions can truly take any form, but the most important thing is that you're all having fun together.

## Ask Your Parents (or Grandparents) about Their Lives at Your Age

Sometimes it can get annoying to hear your elders say, "When I was your age..." This phrase is usually followed by an anecdote about how hard they had it, or how much they worked to get where they are now. Instead of waiting for those stories to arise spontaneously, take the reins and ask a family member out of genuine curiosity what life was like for them when they were your age. It will give them a chance to reminisce about their past and provide you with interesting insight into what life was like during a different time.

 **BONUS TIP**

If possible, ask your elder to show you around to locations of special significance: their old school, first date spots, where they shared their first kiss. It could result in a special experience for both of you.

## Hire a Photographer for a Silly Photo Shoot

A family photo shoot can be a fun, lighthearted way to bond with one another, especially if nobody is too serious about the outcome. A framed photo makes the perfect gift to send to any and all family members. First, find a photographer that shares your vision for the shoot, then work together to set up a makeshift studio where you can take playful pictures in the backyard, collecting various props like bubble machines or a blow-up kiddie pool. Or head to another fun location for your photos, like the skating rink or the park. Regardless of the location you pick, lean in to hamming it up together—picking silly matching outfits and not taking yourselves too seriously. You'll end up with photos that make you laugh every time you see them, and maybe even one that makes the fridge.

## Indulge In Brunch and a Spa Date with Your Parent

When was the last time your parent was indulged with a day at the spa? Show them you're thinking of them by planning a little pampering excursion, whether you've both been dying for a pedicure or they are in need of a deep tissue massage. Start with a fun, boozy brunch together where you can catch up on life, then head over to the spa or salon for a relaxing treatment. If a big spa day isn't in your budget, no worries—try a standard manicure, which can set you back less than $20. No polish is necessary if that isn't your thing.

## Send Your Family Members Handwritten Cards

If you haven't spoken to certain members of your family in a while, show them you still care through spontaneous handwritten notes. You don't need a particular occasion to show that you're thinking of your family, and in fact, it'll feel even more special if there isn't one. There's no need to write anything groundbreaking, either. Just a simple, heartfelt message will do the job. If you have kids, ask them to create a drawing for each letter so that they feel included in the little surprise too.

**BONUS TIP**

Coordinate a rotating family letter lottery: Each participating member creates their own monthly schedule of who they'll be sending their note to. Each month, you'll be able to look forward to receiving a heartfelt message from a different member of your family.

## Go on a Segway Tour Around the City

If you've ever seen groups of tourists zip around your city on Segways, you might have pointed them out as a joke to whoever you were with at the time. But odds are that you actually thought it looked kind of fun—because it is! So, get your family together and explore the sights by way of a Segway tour. You'll have fun leaning in to the kitschy experience and make lasting memories.

## Tackle an Escape Room Together

The ultimate team-building exercise, escape rooms have exploded in popularity because they're a fun way for a group to problem solve together. Because of that popularity, they're also available nearly everywhere. Next time you and your family get together, book an experience at one close by and get ready to solve riddles and find clues to complete your given mission. Your first experience may feel a little disjointed, but come back a couple of times, and you and your family will end up operating as a well-oiled, puzzle-solving machine.

## Purge Your Home and Have a Big Yard Sale

Turn your trash into someone else's treasure with a big collective yard sale. Combining all your family members' stuff into one sale will be more time efficient, and the sheer number of items could help attract some serious customers. Watch as the items that have been collecting dust in your homes find new lives, then use the cash you earned to go out to dinner together.

## Skip the Tent and Try Glamping

One moment you're cracking up with your siblings, and the next, you're in a fight. Getting away from distractions and into nature is a great way to bond, but dealing with the setup of traditional tent camping may detract from your time participating in the more fun parts of camping. Do you want less arguing about tent poles and searching for toilet paper, and more hiking through the woods, swapping ghost stories, and firing up some s'mores? Try glamping! On your next trip, check out the creative glamping setups in the area you're visiting, which may include small cabins, yurts, or bubble tents. You won't have to draw straws over who sets up the tent, and sleeping in a real bed means you'll all wake up refreshed and in the best mood possible to start your day.

## Create a Family Time Capsule

There will never again be a time when you and your family members are the ages you are right now, and in the exact situations you're currently in. Every moment that passes by is precious, so put together a time capsule full of memories to dig up in several years. Kids and adults alike will love it, and anything small enough to fit in the capsule is fair game. What seems like a silly tchotchke today may take on new meaning when it's unearthed by you and your family ten or fifteen years from now. Some ideas for items to include are special photographs, concert and movie tickets, small souvenirs from a recent trip, written letters from each family member, or a current newspaper clipping.

## Set Up Regular Group Video Calls

Do you keep meaning to give your mom a call, but life just gets in the way? Wish you had more time to catch up with your siblings? Hit two birds with one stone by setting up group video calls at regularly scheduled times. Group calls help you to stay in touch with your family and get virtual face time if you aren't all living in the same place. Instead of spending an hour chatting with just one family member, you'll all get to hear about what's going on in several people's lives. Make sure to find a time that generally works for everyone, even if some people aren't able to join every time. Having family time scheduled on your calendar will keep you all connected, even if you're just chatting about your day with them while getting dinner ready.

## Bring the Whole Family Together for Beer Olympics

This one is for adults only. Find the kids a babysitter and get ready for a competitive day of Beer Olympics. For the uninitiated, Beer Olympics is a multigame event where you split into small teams and compete against each other until one team comes out victorious.

### HOW IT WORKS

First, lock down the teams that are competing in the games, splitting all the participants into groups of two to three. Grab the necessary supplies: a whiteboard and dry-erase marker, some basic outdoor banquet tables, cans of beer, and a trophy or prize for the winning team. Next, pick a couple of games like beer pong, flip cup, quarters, or cornhole. Competing teams will rotate through the different games. At the end, the scores are tallied up to find out which team is the winner.

## Join a Family Sports League

Enrolling your kids in sports is one of the best ways to foster their teamwork abilities and to help them understand the importance of community, so why not promote that same mentality within your entire family? Family sports leagues are a fun way to learn how to work together and get competitive with no real-life stakes or repercussions. These leagues are offered for several different sports, such as basketball, soccer, and flag football. Your kids will love seeing a different side of you as you give it your all on the field, and this predominantly social activity offers plenty of chances for both kids and adults to make new friends.

## Create a Rotating Travel Schedule

If your family members are scattered in several different locations, it can be hard to plan times to all see each other. Creating a long-term travel schedule will help simplify visits, make it easier to plan, and ensure that nobody feels left out if most family visits happen in one place.

### HOW IT WORKS

If you'd like to all get together twice a year, create two lists with each person's name on it. One list covers the summer visits, for example, while the other schedules visits during the winter holidays. Plan the first summer visit at the home of the person at the top of that list. The following summer, move down the list to the next locale, and so on. Do the same for the winter list, but stagger the names so that the summer and winter visits don't happen in the same location twice in a row.

## Meet Up with Family Members One-on-One

When was the last time you got dinner with one of your aunts or uncles, just the two of you? Bonding with family when you are all together is one thing, but reaching out to your family members to set up one-on-one time will make them feel like a different level of special, especially if that's something you two haven't done in a while (or ever). It doesn't need to be anything fancy or formal—the important thing is that you're spending time catching up together. If it's a family member who you've never had a deep conversation with, or they're used to seeing you as a kid, this is a great opportunity to learn about each other's lives on a different level and achieve a more meaningful bond.

## Plan a Virtual Game Night

No matter the distance between you, when you set time aside to play games with your family, you help build relationships. You'll make space for jokes and more serious conversation as well as forging memories together. Plus, games are just fun.

### HOW IT WORKS

While it would be awesome to have game night every month, try just one to start during a time when everyone is available to join. Pick at least two games to present to the group and vote on which one to play that evening. If it ends up not being as fun as expected, you already have a backup! Connect to everyone using a platform like Google Hangouts or Zoom, then play games like Heads Up! in which one player races against the clock to guess the correct word based on clues given by the other players.

## Bring Your Kids along to Volunteer

Families who volunteer together don't just benefit from the knowledge that they've done a good deed; they can also feel good about the unique bonds they're building from working together toward a common goal. Showing your kids the impact they can have by volunteering also works to instill a passion for giving back at a young age. The most rewarding work is done when your family has a personal connection to the cause, like volunteering with the elderly after losing a senior family member, or raising money for cancer research while a family member is in remission.

## Take a Family Trip to an All-Inclusive Resort

Family drama, be gone! Sometimes what the family needs when life gets stressful is a little old-fashioned R&R. Give yourselves just that by planning a group trip to somewhere warm and beautiful, where you can spend quality time with each other in a fresh setting without everyday distractions and stressors to get in the way of bonding.

**HOW IT WORKS**

Unless your family is all about it, save the adventurous, off-the-beaten-path destinations for another time, and stick to a place that you know will be a crowd-pleaser for everyone. Logistics are also easier when you book at an all-inclusive resort, where food and drinks are included in the base price and you know you'll always find a spot at the beach. If you're traveling with kids in tow, try finding a resort that offers daycare services. You'll thank yourself later when all the adults want to do is enjoy peace, quiet, and piña coladas at the pool together.

## Have a Backyard Campout

Have your kids been begging for a night spent in a tent, but you're not much of a camper? Meet them halfway by setting up a backyard campout with them. It's the best of both worlds—you don't have to lug a bunch of equipment to an actual campsite, and your kids still get the same outdoorsy experience with cozier blankets and better snacks. You'll all have fun setting up camp together, looking up at the stars, and roasting s'mores (even if you have to go inside to use the stovetop burners).

**BONUS TIP**

Just because you helped them set up the tent doesn't mean you have to sleep out there too. Once they fall asleep, creep back inside and sleep in the comfort of your own bed. When they wake up and smell bacon in the kitchen, they won't care.

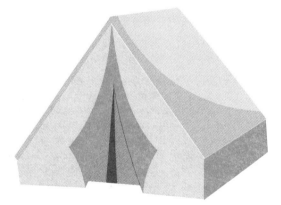

## Send Your Family Members Surprise Treats

There's nothing better than receiving a surprise from someone you love. Show your fam that you're thinking about them by sending little unexpected treats for absolutely no reason. It could really be anything: homemade cookies, store-bought candles, bottles of wine, hand-knitted scarves. Package the gift in a cute bag or box and send it on its way with a nice note. If you live close by, drop off the treats to see the reaction in real time, or mail them to family members who live farther away. Don't be offended if they don't return your act of kindness; if some do, it'll be a nice surprise for you too.

## Go to Family Counseling

Counseling may not sound like a "fun" activity, but it can help you to improve communication and move past issues, allowing you to reconnect and have a better understanding of your family members. This can make way for more solid relationships and more fun in the future. Just like couples' counseling and independent therapy, there doesn't need to be anything wrong to warrant signing up. In fact, going to counseling as a family can be beneficial for all healthy relationships, and it can help strengthen them as well as prevent petty arguments. Counseling also helps families learn how to speak honestly with one another, open up, and share feelings without fear of being judged or persecuted. If you and your family have experienced trauma or loss, it can also be a great tool to collectively learn how to cope and eventually move on.

# CHAPTER 6

# Experience
# the Great Outdoors

After a long week at work, there's nothing more cathartic than getting out into nature, taking that first deep breath of fresh air, and looking down to see you have no cell phone service. You're free!

Sometimes it seems there's never enough time or that you lack the means to spend time outdoors, especially if you live in a big city. As attractive as it sounds to hike through the woods on a Saturday afternoon or jump into a lake, the thought can be daunting if it's not something you do regularly.

This chapter is designed to change your mind about spending time in nature. It's not as involved a process as it may seem. Incorporating simple ways to see more green every week—which is really good for your mental health—is the first step. Before you know it, you'll be pulling your friends in, too, texting them to plan trail runs and convincing them to buy an annual pass to the national parks.

## Plan a Road Trip with Your Best Friends

The next time you decide to take a trip with friends, skip the plane and opt instead for the open road. Road trips are a bonding experience as you chat away in the car and make impromptu stops at lunch and coffee spots or for photo opportunities along the way to your destination. If you're a planner, this activity will give you the opportunity to inject a little joyous spontaneity into your getaway.

**BONUS TIP**

Create a shared playlist for the car ride ahead of time and make sure that everyone gets a chance to show off their favorite songs to the group. Download it to your phone before you head out, so you won't be worried about cell service dead spots along the road.

## Invest In a National Parks Annual Pass

Did you know that you can purchase a full-year pass that covers all the national parks in the US? If you're worried that you won't use it very often, use the purchase as some personal fuel to get out there and experience the beautiful nature of our parks. You'll feel good about playing your part to support the preservation of wild spaces, and you can make plans to visit at least one per season to help with your goal of getting outside more. Plan one national parks trip per season, whether it's just a day of driving through and hiking or an extended campout. You will have several trips to look forward to throughout the year, and each season you'll rack up new parks to tick off your list.

## Find Peace with Bird-Watching

Not every outdoor activity has to boost your adrenaline or be physically strenuous. Next time you're seeking a peaceful way to add more nature to your life, chat with a friend or your partner about the idea of becoming bird-watchers. There are thousands of species of birds to learn about and catch glimpses of in the wild, and you're bound to come across some of them even when walking through a city or on a local trail. Your bird-watching buddy and you will need binoculars and some Google searches to learn about what you can spot in your area. The best bird-watching is done in the morning, which is a perfect time to walk the trails while they're quiet and the weather is mild.

## Forage for Your Own Food

Contrary to popular belief, you don't need to live in the woods to forage for your own kitchen ingredients. Edible vegetables, mushrooms, flowers, leaves, and berries can be found nearly everywhere—even in the larger public parks of cities and towns. The best way to get started is to do ample research to ensure that you don't pick up anything poisonous by accident, and it's suggested to sign up for a foraging class led by an expert before you jump in on your own. Taking a class has double benefits, too, as you could plan future forages with your fellow newbies in the class. Foraging is a fun and unexpected way to get out into nature, and you can impress friends by preparing dishes with your new hyper-local ingredients.

## Join a Community Garden

If you don't have a backyard of your own, check to see if your neighborhood has a community garden—a shared space where you can grow herbs, fruits, vegetables, flowers, or any other plants in a designated plot. The act of gardening and physically working with the earth is proven to reduce stress and make you happy. Joining your community garden also gives you access to a whole new group of possible friends who share your green thumb enthusiasm. Plan times to visit the garden with one or more of your new friends, or set up times to share seeds or cuttings for propagation.

## Find the Nearest Natural Body of Water and Jump In

This one is self-explanatory, but there are so many ways to have fun with it. No matter where you live, it's pretty much guaranteed that there is a river, lake, or ocean within driving distance of your home. This weekend, instead of trying to plan something more involved like a day of water sports or renting a boat, make a simple plan to get out there and enjoy being outside. All you need are snacks, hydration, friends, and a towel to get the day started. Oh, and don't forget to bring your sunscreen along too.

## Adopt a Furry Friend

Have you been thinking of adopting a pet for years now? If so, take this as your sign to go for it! Having a canine best friend provides you with a built-in excuse to get outside multiple times a day for walks, to run around in the park, and to generally be more active. Bringing your dog to the park solo is a great way to make new connections, too, or you can set up times to walk dogs with your other pet-owning friends during your lunch hour or after work. On weekends, take your pets to hit the trails or to cool down at the river.

## Visit Your Local Winery

Wineries may not come immediately to mind when you think about the great outdoors, but they still count! Usually removed from the city, wineries cover gorgeous acres of land covered in greenery—the keys to receiving the happy brain benefits you get from being in nature. Instead of just heading to the tasting room, though, make sure to sign you and your friends up for a full tour of the property. Walking around the vineyard for the afternoon will give you the perfect dose of nature, and you'll gain a new appreciation for the product you'll all enjoy afterward.

### Learn How to Build a Campfire and Pitch a Tent

On group camping trips, isn't there usually one experienced person who always ends up building the fire or pitching the tents? Next time, before you go, express your enthusiasm to learn from them so you can help out on future trips. They'll appreciate having someone else along to set up those foundations, and you'll learn some helpful outdoor skills that you can use for the rest of your life—win-win! If you've been itching to go camping and none of your friends are well-versed outdoor adventurers, try looking for classes in practical skills. Supplement the classes with learning other skills like archery to bring out your inner Katniss Everdeen.

### Embrace the Outdoors in a Creative Way

Next time you set out on a tromp through nature, take time to slow down your pace and really take in the world around you. Bring a sketch pad along, and ask your hiking mate to bring one too. You can take turns picking spots to settle in for a few minutes to creatively interpret your surroundings. It's your choice if you'd like to share your sketches or keep them private. It's fun seeing how differently people see the same thing.

**BONUS TIP**

Make your art stops even more enjoyable by bringing along a picnic. Grab items that can pack up well without much chance of leaking or spilling, like charcuterie board elements, sandwiches, bottled iced teas, and fruit. Line the walls of your backpack with malleable ice packs and make sure to include an ample amount of napkins, paper plates, and cutlery.

## Opt for Trail Running Instead of Your Normal Neighborhood Route

Need a way to motivate yourself to go farther on your regular runs? Add some interest and variety by changing your go-to neighborhood route to one that brings you closer to nature. Bring different friends who might challenge you in unusual ways too. Have one friend who's all about speed, and another one who focuses on endurance? Alternate your invites, enticing them with trail runs. It doesn't matter where you live: You may have a forested area nearby, a state or national park, a bird sanctuary, or even a large public park. The point is to get away from the stop signs and slow-moving pedestrians and into nature.

## Make the Park Your New Gym

By using the outdoors as your gym, you can get your fitness on and experience nature at the same time. If you can usually be found on the cardio machines, try going for a run around the park instead, and do your floor routine right there on the grass. Weightlifters can utilize their own body weight and playground equipment to do pull-ups, leg raises, and more. Classic workout moves like squats and lunges are definitely options at the park, and they're perfect to alternate with sprints across the lawn.

**BONUS TIP**

Hit the park early in the morning when there aren't as many people to get in your way as you run around. The weather will also be more agreeable if you're working out in the summer months.

## Spend an Afternoon Fishing

You don't technically need an excuse to spend a lazy afternoon hanging out at the pier or lake, but fishing is a pretty good one nonetheless. If you've never tried fishing before, it's easy to pick up the basics quickly, and if you have any friends who fish, they'd undoubtedly love to teach you. If not, hire a fishing guide and bring a group who wants to learn alongside you. Fishing is a community-oriented hobby, with enthusiasts to be found all over the country. Tap in to that network to make new friends and further your knowledge on everything from sustainable practices to local marine life.

## Get a Group Together for a Farm Visit

Take your farmers' market obsession to new heights by coordinating a trip to a local you-pick farm. Regardless of the season, there's bound to be something ripe for the picking: apples, pumpkins, blueberries, tomatoes, you name it! Because of their seasonality, farm visits are an activity you can revisit time and time again throughout the year, as activities vary so drastically. During the fall, you may want to wander through a corn maze or hop on a hayride with friends; come winter, you may choose a holiday tree to bring home with your partner.

## Become a Member of Your Local Arboretum

Like becoming a member of your favorite art museum, joining the community of your local arboretum or botanical garden not only means you get in free for a year; it also ensures that you can rest easy, knowing your money went to supporting a good cause that protects green space in your neighborhood.

**BONUS TIP**

Instead of saving a trip to the garden for an entire weekend afternoon, make time for a quick nature walk on your lunch or afternoon break. Bring a friend or the kids to take in the much-needed serenity of the park during a time when you won't find Sunday crowds. It's guaranteed you'll return to your computer with a much clearer mind after giving yourself that break in screen time.

## Join a Hiking Group

When it comes to any outdoor activity, safety should come first. Not only is it more fun to hike with a group, but it's safer as well. Join an outdoors group to meet more people who love to spend time in nature and to secure hiking buddies for any time you feel like hitting the trails. You can easily find such groups online. Once you join, you'll find lots of resources and events, like local trail guides, group hikes, and subsets of group members who plan volunteer days or have specialized interests like kayaking, bike riding, or rock climbing.

## Commit to Daily Morning Walks

Rev up your daily step count with morning walks that challenge you to avoid that snooze button. The early morning is the perfect time to squeeze in some nature time, whether you're just staring up at the trees in your neighborhood or driving over to your favorite birding spot with binoculars at the ready. By the time you sit down at your desk or head in to start the workday, you'll already feel massively more accomplished and in a better state of mind than if you had kept your head on your pillow. Bonus points if you're able to get your partner or a friend up to come with—share the wealth! Having someone join you keeps you accountable, since it's so much easier to talk yourself into "just fifteen more minutes" when it's a solo plan.

## Go Horseback Riding

When thinking about spending more time outdoors, horseback riding might not be your first thought. But it allows you to explore trails from a new perspective and to engage your mind and body in a different way than you are typically used to. Where there are hiking trails, especially in more rural areas, there are usually horses nearby. A quick Internet search should yield options for places to take a horse out for the afternoon, whether alone or with a guide. Besides the opportunity to bond with a beautiful, intelligent animal, horseback riding on a scenic trail is also a unique date option if you're looking for something new to try with your partner.

## Have a Neighborhood Water Balloon Fight

Because of entertaining distractions like gaming and social media, it can be tough to convince kids to spend time outdoors. One foolproof way is to entice them with something engaging and competitive, like a big water balloon fight in the backyard or park on a hot summer day. Water balloon fights are an inexpensive but exciting way to spend your afternoon, especially when you follow them up with a simple grilled lunch and some fresh fruit. If it's not summertime, rake up a pile of leaves to jump in, or have a light-hearted snowball fight.

## Participate in Trail Cleanup Days

We've all had it happen—finding a beautiful trail, beach, or field only to realize that it's littered with trash and generally unkept. Get a group together to clean up an area on your own or coordinate with a nonprofit that leads regular volunteer cleanups.

**HOW IT WORKS**

If you're planning your own cleanup effort, start by choosing a local trail, creek, or neighborhood block to focus on. If there aren't trash receptacles nearby, contact your local disposal company to find out about drop-off points. Try to keep your group within ten people, and make sure everyone stays near the trail with their cell phones turned on. Cleanup materials can be bought cheap, and you can find whole kits, including gloves and grabber tools, at outdoor stores like REI.

## Get PADI-Certified

Hobbies don't have to be solitary or something that keeps you inside all day. Choose a hobby that brings you outdoors more often and can include the participation of friends and loved ones, like scuba diving. You don't even need to live by the water in order to take a course to become PADI-certified. In most places, courses are available where you can learn how to scuba dive in a swimming pool. Once you have the certification under your belt, plan a fun trip to put your newfound skills to good use.

## Treat Yourself to Some New Gear As an Incentive

Just as a new favorite outfit may entice you to find a party or dinner to attend, new outdoor gear can be an incentive to plan that next camping trip. Scour sales at big-name outdoor retailers for deals on the basics like boots and cozy sleeping bags, or niche outdoor gear that may inspire you to try something new. If you're trying to cook more outdoors, a portable grill plate and a sturdy pan will get you started. Even a French press and tin mugs will help put you in that camping state of mind. For creating a moment of ultimate relaxation while outdoors, another useful purchase may be a quality hammock to lounge in while reading a book or taking a nap.

## Plan Your Next Dinner with Friends Outdoors

There's something magical about a meal enjoyed al fresco, and it's actually easier to plan than you might think. Whether you choose to enjoy a meal in your backyard or head to a public park, it's all about preparation. If you have a large enough outdoor space to host in, barbecued skewers and seasonal vegetables make an easy crowd-pleaser meal, especially when paired with bread and a large pitcher of something refreshing. For dinner at the park, try bringing cold items that are filling, like sandwiches on baguettes and fresh fruit.

### BONUS TIP

To create an even more magical vibe at your dinner, add a vase of branches or flowers in the middle of the table, a simple linen or cotton table runner, a string of fairy lights, and a portable dessert to enjoy afterward, like cookies or brownies.

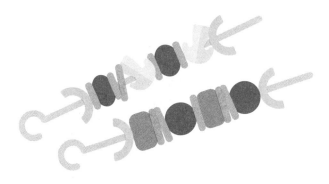

## Create a Daily Step Goal

Did you know that you can track steps on your smartphone even if you don't have a fancy fitness tracker or Apple Watch? Tracking your daily steps keeps you accountable and staying active. A good goal to start with is 10,000 steps per day, which can be reached by giving yourself movement breaks throughout the day. Add movement to your day by walking around your neighborhood, lunging across your home or apartment, jogging to get a cup of coffee, taking your dog to the park, running errands on foot, taking public transportation to meet friends, or going for a stroll after dinner.

## Enroll in Outdoor Workout Classes

Running around the park will definitely keep you fit, but sometimes the structure of a workout class is what you need to stay active on a regular basis. Classes help vary your activity, which will ensure you don't eventually hit a physical plateau. For the next month, try planning a schedule of classes that take place outdoors, like HIIT (high-intensity interval training), Zumba dance, and yoga. Many independent fitness instructors conduct their classes in public parks, and some fitness studios have a private outdoor area as well. Either way, you'll receive the double benefits of more outdoor time and more physical activity to keep both your mind and body happy.

## Hit the Water on a Kayak

A surprisingly versatile way to spend more time outdoors is by way of kayak. You can go for a leisurely paddle one day and hit the rapids the next (if you dare). Kayaking is also really good for you. It helps build up cardiac strength, lowers your stress levels, serves as a full-body workout, and is almost always more fun when you bring a friend along to help paddle and keep you company. If you don't have room to store a kayak, consider an inflatable kayak, which fits easily into the trunk of a car. Or search around your area for companies that rent kayaks out for an afternoon.

## Challenge Yourself to Take a Backpacking Trip

Spending an afternoon conquering a challenging hike is one thing—but what about one that lasts multiple days? If you want to push yourself to the next level, backpacking can do just that. A multiday backpacking trip is also a great way to connect with nature, as you explore miles of backcountry in a way you couldn't possibly accomplish on a typical hike.

### HOW IT WORKS

If this is your first attempt at backpacking, remember that it's a marathon and not a sprint. Pick a well-marked trail that is only a few miles round trip with a moderate amount of elevation gain. Don't forget to bring all the necessary gear, backup meals that are easy to prepare, and plenty of protein-rich snacks for when you get hungry on the trail. Mark on your map where you plan to settle for the night, and check that you have all necessary permits and that there will be a water source nearby.

## Take Advantage of Seasonal Activities

If you live in a place with marked differences in seasonal weather, take advantage! With the start of each season comes a whole new range of outdoor activities, from beach going in the summer to snowman building in the winter. During fleeting seasons like fall and spring, it's even more special to get outside and witness the natural world change right before your eyes. Certain hikes are also more fun and scenic during a particular season. During summer months, seek out hikes that culminate at lakes and waterfalls, while hiking to a peak or a dramatic overlook is usually the most gorgeous in the fall.

## Catch an Outdoor Concert or Show

It doesn't matter that you're surrounded by a bunch of other people—an al fresco concert still counts as an outdoor activity! Plenty of outdoor venues offer an experience that feels less like a traditional concert and more like a picnic with live music. Not only are lawn tickets usually the most affordable option at an outdoor concert, but they also give you the chance to actually chat and mingle with the friends you came with—double bonus.

**BONUS TIP**

Check to see if the venue allows outside food and beverages, as many do. You and your friends can go in together on a picnic basket of goodies to bring with you to the show, like finger sandwiches and chips or even a charcuterie board and a bottle of vino.

## Create a Nature Scavenger Hunt for the Whole Family

Kids always seem to have more fun when they can grab things they're not supposed to, right? Engage their love of nature by creating a scavenger hunt for the next time you plan a walk, which will finally allow them to pick up that acorn they keep trying to pocket.

### HOW IT WORKS

Start by picking a location—maybe a botanical garden, park, or trail—and take notice of what you can easily find there. If it's spring, are there plenty of flowers around? If it's winter, is the ground covered in pinecones? Next, create a list of things for your kid to find. It can include a couple of objects to take home as well as things to draw or take pictures of. You can find editable scavenger hunt sheets for purchase on sites like *Etsy*.

## Gift Your Kid Their First Camera

Got little ones? It's never too early to kick-start their love of nature. Once they get old enough to use a camera, give them a disposable point-and-shoot. They'll have tons of fun capturing the world from their point of view, and the images they capture are mementos you'll be able to hold on to forever. Have them take photos of whatever catches their eye in the backyard, or go on short nature walks together equipped with their new camera. Spending time outside will spark their curiosity in a way that an iPad never could. Not to mention it will tire them out too.

## Bring Some Plant Babies Home from a Nursery

When you can't get outside to experience nature, the next best thing is to bring it inside with you! Plants provide many benefits for both your mental and physical health. Owning houseplants has been shown to help with everything from mood improvement to combating fatigue and boosting creativity. Besides that, they brighten up and enliven any space, and there are tons of varieties that flourish under any kind of light conditions.

**BONUS TIP**

Before you go to the nursery, take a few photos of your space during peak daylight hours. It'll be helpful to show those photos to the experts who can help you pick out the perfect plants for your space, which will depend on the amount of room and natural light you have.

## Take Your Reading or Work Outdoors

If you almost instantly fall asleep while reading in bed, or you're experiencing that dreaded midday work slump, it might be time for a little change of scenery. One easy way to accomplish this is simply to head outside for some fresh air. If you have a backyard or front porch where your Wi-Fi coverage extends, that's ideal, but public parks and cafés with outdoor space offer free Internet connection as well. Sometimes all your brain needs is that hit of fresh oxygen to click back on, so it'll serve you (and your productivity levels) well to give it just that.

# CHAPTER 7

# Meet
## New Friends

A common misconception is that it's hard to make friends as an adult. But everyone wants to make connections. Between the stressors of work, paying bills, and possibly raising children, friends are a shoulder to lean on and a safe place to vent.

It's true that creating and maintaining those connections takes work, but there's nothing in this world worth having that doesn't take a bit of time and effort. The cardinal rule of making new friends as a grown-up is to simply put yourself out there and not feel embarrassed about doing so.

If that sounds a bit terrifying, this chapter is here to help! It's full of fun and easy methods for making new connections and strengthening the ones you already have, no matter what stage of life you're in right now.

## Join a Running Group

If you don't consider yourself a runner, that's only because you haven't gotten started! Running with others not only keeps you accountable; it provides opportunities to make new friends too. You're less likely to cancel a run when you're planning to meet people and it's become a social activity. Studies even show that runners who are part of a club or group tend to feel more supported (both during and outside of the run!), and that people make meaningful friendships within these groups.

If you're not sure where to start, check out Road Runners Club of America to see if they have groups in your area. Another good place to check out is your local sports club or running shops—they likely have information on clubs or groups that you can join and may even offer their own.

## Volunteer at Your Local Animal Shelter

Volunteering offers an easy opportunity to meet new people. If you're an animal lover, the local shelter is a place where you can give your time to a cause you're passionate about while also making new connections with people who share that passion.

To get started, plan to devote a realistic amount of time that doesn't overwhelm you or your schedule, like once a week or even once a month. Regardless of how often you're able to volunteer, make the time worth it! Many organizations create chat boards or *Facebook* groups for their volunteers, making it even easier to strike up conversations and make new connections.

## Put Yourself Out There (Digitally)

If you're yearning for more quality connections in your life, you're certainly not the only one. Whether you're new to your city or have friends moving out of it, it never hurts to add more good people to your social roster. One of the best ways to do that is by utilizing the power of the Internet, whether you're tapping in to features like Bumble BFF or local *Facebook* groups, or posting a video call-out for friends on TikTok. It may sound a bit crazy at first, but it's guaranteed you'll end up patting yourself on the back for taking the chance to push yourself out of your comfort zone.

## Sign Up for a Creative Course

Get in touch with your hidden creative side by signing up for a multiweek artistic course, whether it leads you to learn the basics of pottery making, glass blowing, painting, creative writing, or even improv. Whichever craft sounds the most interesting to you, the key is committing to it for a designated span of time—not just a single evening.

Building your newfound skills each week with the same small group of people is an amazing bonding experience as you learn together through trial and error. Make plans to get together as a group directly after your last class to raise a glass to all you have learned, and to exchange contact info if you'd like to stay in touch.

## Try Solo Dining, or Take a Seat at the Bar

Always exercise caution and remain aware of your surroundings while dining or drinking solo, but with that being said, you can meet a lot of new people while solo dining—whether that means a new group of friends or a romantic prospect. Choose a restaurant or bar in an area that you're already familiar with and take a seat at the bar. Order your favorite drink, strike up a conversation with the bartender, and keep yourself open to the possibility of meeting new people.

**BONUS TIP**

Remember that a genuine compliment can go a long way! If you see potential friends at the bar, start with a small compliment or a polite question and see where the conversation goes from there.

## Take Up a Social Side Hustle

Does your day job require you to be strapped to a desk for the better part of the morning and afternoon? Pick a part-time side hustle that does the opposite, like bartending at your favorite watering hole by night or walking dogs around town in the morning. Don't get the chance to be creative at work? Join a knitting circle or try jewelry making with friends, then launch your new small business on a site like *Etsy*! If something immediately came to your mind while reading this, maybe that is your internal cue that you should take a chance on bringing that dream to life. Once you've decided on what your side hustle might entail, check out some blogs and articles to read tips and personal stories from people who have already launched a similar gig.

## Learn a New Language

Whether you're a polyglot who needs a refresher or you're looking to get in touch with your cultural heritage for the first time through language, taking a language course or joining a foreign language group allows you to learn something new and meet fun people all at once.

For those intent on becoming fluent in a new language but are also on a budget, sign up for an online learning subscription like Rosetta Stone or Duolingo, then enhance your lessons with in-person group meetups that will help you become fluent quickly.

**BONUS TIP**

Once you have the basics down, invite some of your new language-learning friends to a restaurant that prepares the food of the culture you're exploring. Try to go the whole meal only speaking in that language —it'll get easier after the second round of drinks.

## Bring Your Dog to the Park

Meet other dog lovers by bringing yours to off-leash hours at your local park. Most of the other pet owners there will be from the immediate vicinity, so there's a good chance any new friends you make will be within a few minutes' walk or drive away. Next time you head over, bring treats with you, making sure to ask first before you feed any to the other pups. Your neighbors will appreciate it, and it'll provide an excuse to strike up a conversation.

## Bond over Music at a Show

If you've never attended a concert on your own, now is the time. It's honestly great because you can see any artist you like without worrying about getting friends on board. That niche indie band you have on repeat but no one else seems to know about yet? Go ahead and book your ticket. When it comes to the possibility of meeting new friends (or someone special) at a show, it's best to choose a smaller, intimate venue that isn't seated. While there, concentrate on enjoying yourself, whether you meet people or not. Music has the unique ability to connect people, though, so chances are you'll at least find a fun group to have a drink with and bop along to the tunes.

**BONUS TIP**

Before you go, have fun playing around with your outfit. Choosing something you feel good in will give you a nice confidence boost that'll make the night feel all the more special.

## Volunteer at Your Favorite Workout Studio

Did you know that most local workout studios are able to function because of volunteer workers? This fact is not widely advertised, but those in the know can volunteer in exchange for free classes. It's a win-win situation if it works for you—getting to know the other staff members and regulars at the studio and then being able to come in on your own time to do your workout. Most volunteers will be in charge of things like guest check-in, studio cleanup pre- and post-class, and general maintenance. To check whether your favorite studio offers a similar program, just ask at the front desk, or send them an email!

## Attend Book Signings or Local Talks

Among the plethora of reasons to support your local bookshop are the events and book signings they host, often for free. Check their website or, better yet, just stop in to take a look at their upcoming calendar. Of course, not all bookstores offer events, but many at least host authors for exclusive readings to celebrate the launch of a new book. Some even take it a step beyond with book clubs, poetry slams, and more. Attending these solo gives you the chance to meet other bibliophiles in your area, who not only share your love for books but an interest in a particular author as well.

**BONUS TIP**

If your local bookstore doesn't offer any event programming, try joining a book club instead, which will help you connect with new people and find even more awesome books to read. No matter where you're based, you'll be able to find a book club that suits your reading style.

## Try Remote Working at a Coffee Shop

This one works best for those who work from home but could also be a once-a-week option for office workers who work from home on a part-time basis. While the comfort of home makes it an ideal office situation for some, it can also be tough to stay motivated throughout the day when your bed is so close by. Studies have also shown that it's healthy to keep your leisure space and work-space separate.

Check on your favorite maps app or a café's website to see if they offer free Wi-Fi, then head over and set up at a communal table if possible. A simple request to your fellow café goers to help plug in your charger could lead to conversation.

## Become a Yes Person

It might sound a bit cliché, but simply saying yes more often can lead to some awesome changes in your life. Becoming a yes person helps you adopt a personal growth mindset and signals to friends old and new that you're their go-to person when they want to try something fun. Whether it's something small, like waking up early to grab a morning coffee, or something more involved, like requesting time off work to take that long weekend trip you've been talking about for ages, saying yes can help jump-start positive progress in your life. To start, pick a time frame—like one week or one month—during which you commit to saying yes to every invite, big or small.

## Initiate Hangouts with Your Colleagues

If most conversations with your colleagues revolve around things like that four p.m. meeting you need to prep for or when the next report is due, it's time to switch things up. Of course you should always keep interactions professional, but there's nothing wrong with making friends with your coworkers. To introduce more casual conversation, simply ask about someone's day or send them a work-related meme. Once you identify a colleague you seem to share some interests with, go ahead and initiate a coffee or drink.

**BONUS TIP**

If you don't feel comfortable reaching out about a solo hang, ask your manager about facilitating a whole team happy hour. They'll be impressed that you took the initiative to ask, and it'll present you with an opportunity to get to know your team on another level outside of the office.

## Set a Personal Goal for Networking Events

Networking events can be nerve-racking, but they get easier the more you attend them. Challenge yourself to set a personal goal for how many you want to attend during any one period of time, like once a quarter or once every month. Alternatively, make a goal to gather ten business cards at each gathering. Keeping a goal like this in mind makes it easier to navigate these kinds of events.

## Ask People Out on Friend Dates

Spending time with your friends in a group setting is always a fun time, but it's the solo hangs that really facilitate closeness. Spending the day with one friend can be a next-level bonding experience that allows you two to share personal stories, talk candidly  about work and relationships, and get to know one another on a deeper level. Whether you're seeking to strengthen the bonds you already have, or create ones with a new friend, don't be afraid to reach out to plan a friend date.

**BONUS TIP**

If you're planning a date with someone you know quite well, a whole day of activities, a weekend trip, or even a low-key hangout at your home are perfect options. For spending time with newer friends, try something like going for dinner at a restaurant you've been wanting to try or attending an event that you'd both enjoy.

## Follow Up with That Potential Friend

We've all been there—you connect with someone new at a party, event, or elsewhere, and you both promise to stay in touch but never do. Sometimes it's fear or a busy schedule that prevents you from reaching out, or maybe you're simply hoping they're the one who contacts you first. Next time, set aside the reasons to not reach out, and just do it! They'll doubtless be happy to hear from you (otherwise they wouldn't have shared their contact info), and now you can concentrate on planning something fun to do together rather than wondering if or when you might hear from them.

## Plan a Hangout with Another Couple

If you and your partner have busy schedules, it's tough enough to find time to spend together, so finding even more time to spend with friends can be a challenge. One solution is to find other couple friends you both like to spend time with—you can do all the fun activities you like to do as a duo with friends, and you won't feel guilty putting on a little PDA as you might around single friends.

### HOW IT WORKS

If you don't already have coupled friends to embark on these adventures with, think about expanding your circle. Consider attending a dance class, cooking class, or group hike as a couple, making a concerted effort to be social and chat up other couples while you're there. The people you meet will share at least one of your interests, so you'll have something in common from the start.

## Strike Up a Convo at School Pickup Time

Picking your kids up from school can be a stressful time: the traffic, finding parking, small humans running around and shouting. Next time, carve out an extra thirty minutes and head there early, even if you need to take a call on the drive over. You'll miss a big chunk of the traffic, find that convenient spot faster, and have time to socialize with other parents who have begun lining up to collect their little ones. Be open to conversing with some parents you haven't spoken to before—you never know who you might end up connecting with, and there's a possibility you could find a new playmate for your kid too.

## Meet Your Neighbors

If you recently moved into a new home or apartment building, there's no reason why you shouldn't become friends with some of your neighbors. Living so close to your friends is enough of an incentive to do so, and will also come in handy if you need someone to look after your pets or plants when you go on vacation. Neighbors can also give you tips on your new local community.

### HOW IT WORKS

Bring over a plate of cookies or other goodies to make a good first impression and to also get a lay of the land in terms of who lives where. If you'd still like a chance to get to know everyone, throw a housewarming party and invite them all.

## Find a Workout Buddy

Sometimes finding new friends feels even harder than perfecting your push-up, but the good thing is that you can actually work on both goals at the same time. Making a new friend in your workout class means that you get a built-in workout buddy who can keep you accountable and try new workouts with you.

**HOW IT WORKS**

If your goal is to meet people, sign up for classes in studios that you know won't be dark and loud, and seek out those that focus on partnered or group exercises. Arrive at least ten minutes early to class, and then ask someone who looks friendly if they've ever taken the class before. This is an easy icebreaker. Remember, most of the people taking these classes are probably hoping to make friends out of the experience just as much as you are.

## Make Social Media Friends

You've heard the cliché about "sliding into" someone's direct messages (DMs). But it can actually be a good way to make new connections in your area (and it doesn't need to be romantic). You don't even need to meet up with your social media friend in person if you don't feel comfortable doing so.

**HOW IT WORKS**

Think about the things you're interested in: Maybe it's fashion, cooking, or art. Those are great points of connection, and searching for those interests on social platforms is one place to start. Be mindful about what you post, too, making an effort to share photos or articles that pertain to your interests. Your potential new friend can click on your profile and easily see how your interests might align.

## Take a Course

If you've been feeling extra "meh" at work lately and think it might be time for a career switch up, feel out your options by taking a class at your local university. It's never too late to learn a new skill or make a necessary change in your life, and night or weekend courses are available in pretty much any subject you can think of, from mechanical engineering or finance to video production or architecture. Continuing education classes also offer the chance to meet new people. It's easy to form a connection when you're working toward the same goal. Consider starting a study group to meet up with your fellow students outside of class.

## Join a Planning Committee

There are tons of ways to feel like you're a part of your community by getting involved in local event planning. You may prefer philanthropic events like community cleanups and can drives, or you can seek out planning committees that organize fun local activities like fairs, markets, and shows. Whatever your interests are, you can find some way to get involved, which opens you up to a whole new network of possible friends and connections.

## Plan Parent-and-Child Play Dates

Becoming a parent doesn't mean the end of your social life. In fact, it could be a time to add even more friends to your social roster. While you may not have as much time to connect with your nonparent friends, just remember that any play date you set up for your kid(s) can mean social time for you too. With that in mind, plan some group play dates to see not only who your child begins to form bonds with, but which parents you get along with the best too.

## Start a Compliment Challenge

One easy way to strike up any conversation with a stranger is to start by giving them a well-intentioned (and non-creepy) compliment. Receiving a genuine, unexpected compliment is such a good feeling, and knowing that you made someone's day will make you feel great in return. Challenge yourself to give out one compliment per day—while you're waiting to board the bus, in line at a coffee shop, or in other similar scenarios. It also helps to follow the compliment up with a related question that can help to facilitate a conversation, like "I love that shirt. Where did you get it?" If the person is on the run and the exchange is quick, don't be discouraged! Each time you step outside of your social comfort zone is a chance to keep growing.

## Become a Board Member

If you're a professional looking for a way to meet other successful people while also giving back, becoming the board member of a nonprofit is the perfect way to accomplish both goals. Becoming part of a nonprofit board means you'll most likely attend monthly meetings, field occasional calls, and help plan events to raise money for the cause. It's usually not an overwhelming amount of time to put in, and you will be able to tap in to the special camaraderie among members. Other perks include broadening your skill set and building your resume.

**BONUS TIP**

Make sure to apply for a board position that aligns well with your values. If you already volunteer with a nonprofit, reach out to your volunteer supervisor about opportunities to become more involved.

## Meet Up with Friends of Friends

Moving to a new place can be difficult, especially when you don't know anyone there. If you find yourself in this situation, don't despair! One of the best ways to make new friends (new location or not) is to tap in to the network of people you already know. If you are in a new place, think of people you know who might have gone to school there or previously lived in the area. They probably still have connections they can introduce you to. If nobody is coming to mind, post an announcement of your move on your social media accounts, asking for local recommendations. Chances are anyone who is familiar with the area will let you know which bars and restaurants to check out, as well as friends they know who live there.

## Try a Solo Activity

The thought of going somewhere or trying something by yourself can be daunting. It's natural to worry about feeling lonely, but it's all about an attitude shift. Going solo to a restaurant, gallery, museum, café, or anywhere else is actually very empowering and can lead you to meet new people who share your interests. If you head into the situation with an open mind and heart, and plan to be sociable once you arrive, you'll be seen as much more approachable than if you came with a band of friends.

**BONUS TIP**

Going to a show or opening by yourself also gives you the power to arrive and leave whenever you choose. If you're nervous about starting conversations with strangers, remember that you can have as little or as much social interaction as you feel comfortable with.

## Utilize *Facebook* Groups

Whether you're into running, knitting, or knitting while running, there is most likely a *Facebook* group that is all about that. A simple search will turn up results, and then all you have to do is join and start connecting. There are also lots of social media groups that are aimed at making connections in a particular city, with connection points as broad as simply living there, to more niche online communities that meet up to cook together or post local events and housing opportunities. Once you find a group to join, try to be intentional about how you communicate. Introduce yourself with some background information about who you are, what you do, and what kind of connections you'd like to form. One major thing to avoid is oversharing—don't spam the group by posting too frequently.

## Reconnect with School Friends

Regardless of how much time has passed since you've seen your old friends from school, you share special memories and experiences that nobody else will ever understand in the same way. It's never too late to rekindle some of those friendships from your past or even spark new ones with acquaintances you didn't get to know well enough back in the day. It's natural for friend groups to be split up by distance and conflicting schedules. What that also means, though, is that people from your high school or college have been moving around for some time, and a few of them most likely relocated to where you are now too. Sure, it can feel weird to reach out after all this time, but the person on the receiving end will likely be glad you did.

## Work on Nurturing Your Existing Friendships

You may feel like you have no strong relationships and that the only solution is to create new bonds. If your current friendships feel one-sided or toxic, then perhaps that is the best route to take. But if it feels like you and your friends have fallen out of touch, it may just take some extra effort to show you care.

### HOW IT WORKS

You don't need as much time as you might think to show someone you want to keep close. Set regular reminders to send your friends short messages to say you're thinking about them, or send them something funny that they might enjoy. At your next get-together, make sure to put your next hangout on the calendar, even if it's a month later.

## Make Friends from Different Generations

When you're at school, you get used to making friends your own age, but as you get older, age doesn't mean as much. When you insist on making connections only with those in your age group, you miss out on a whole spectrum of possible friendships. Friends born in generations other than your own, whether younger or older, can teach you so much about the world from a different perspective. Challenge yourself to think outside of the box when it comes to the kind of person you'd find a friend in. A great place to make these kinds of intergenerational connections is at work, where you already know you can connect with people through shared professional interests. Next time you run into friendly neighbors, try striking up a conversation to learn more about them and their story—you never know what you may have in common!

# CHAPTER 8

# Seek More
## Thrills

Ruts—everyone falls into them once in a while. Once you're in one, it's hard to imagine pulling yourself out of it. When all your days seem to be running together and your brain feels foggy, like you're running on autopilot, sometimes what you need is a kick start.

You may not think that skydiving or zip-lining is a healthy thing to do, but sometimes it actually is (for our brains, at least). Any thrill-seeking situation triggers a response in the bundle of neurons at the base of our brains called the amygdala. This part of the brain, responsible for assessing the unknown, floods your system with the rush of dopamine, adrenaline, and endorphins that make thrills so worth the scare. Your body and brain are hyper aware, bringing you fully into the present moment.

This chapter delves further into the joy of the thrill, with examples on how you can incorporate more regular excitement into your life. It covers ways to challenge yourself physically, like taking archery lessons or trying a flying trapeze, as well as ways to overcome mental blocks that prevent you from getting a raise at work or landing your dream mentor. You can wave goodbye to that rut now.

## Grab a Buddy and Leap Out of a Plane

In an effort to gauge how fearless or daring you are, a classic question that always comes up is whether or not you've gone (or would go) skydiving. It makes sense—it's an activity that is definitely not for the faint of heart. Sometimes literally pushing yourself out of your comfort zone—or out of a plane—can make you feel empowered to do the same in other areas of your life, and whether you decide to bring a friend or significant other, it's certainly a bonding experience. If you're really feeling nervous, remember that skydiving is actually safer than it seems. To give you some perspective, one is more likely to die from being struck by lightning or from a dog bite than from skydiving.

## Get Competitive at Go-Karting

There's nothing wrong with a little friendly competition, which is exactly what you get with go-karting. For a totally safe dose of adrenaline rush, grab a few friends and head over to your local go-kart park for a few laps around the course. Go-karting is available both indoors and outdoors, so you can go any time of the year. It doesn't require any previous experience or even a driver's license, so kids can join in too. If you're going with friends, make it even more fun by adding a little incentive. The person in last place has to buy the winner a drink or an ice cream cone.

## Create a List of What Is Holding You Back

The growth that comes from challenging yourself can come in all different forms. The first step to start tackling what it is that's holding you back is to figure out what you're afraid of. Once you determine what's holding you back, whether it's your demanding job or a fear of rejection, you can start working on how to live your best life.

### HOW IT WORKS

Begin by writing down a list in a stream of consciousness. Don't overthink it too much; simply write down whatever comes to mind when thinking about possible roadblocks in your life. Take a look at your list the next day with a fresh mind and think more critically about why those things came to your mind immediately—then you can start to tackle them head-on. Whether your first step is to seek a physical thrill or one that involves your job or a relationship, this is your time to go for it.

## Soar Through the Trees with Zip-Lining

Some say that when you fly in your dreams, it's symbolic of releasing yourself from whatever it is that holds you back. Well, zip-lining is like doing that but IRL. Securely hanging from a suspended cable, you literally zip through the air from one landing to another, taking in the sights around you from a totally new vantage point. While zip-lining is fun to do while traveling, you can also do it almost anywhere. Glide down the side of a mountain, breeze through a treetop canopy, or whiz by a waterfall. It's guaranteed to be a rush anywhere and anytime you do it.

## Try Public Speaking

For some people, the idea of public speaking is a nightmare. The best way to improve your public-speaking skills is to practice them, and luckily there are organizations like Toastmasters, where you can practice with other people who share the same goal. You may be surprised by how empowering it feels to have your voice heard!

### BONUS TIP

If speaking to a crowd seems terrifying, try speaking up in your next work meeting first. Read over the meeting materials earlier that day and write down a few bullet points of what you want to say and why. Coming prepared will give you the boost of confidence you need to speak up. Challenge yourself to make a comment or ask a question once a week, and see what happens. The results may surprise you in the best way.

## Try White-Water Rafting

White-water rafting is one of the most thrilling activities to get your adrenaline pumping. Take it slow and go with a guide if you're a novice, but once you get the hang of it, lean in to the exhilarating feeling of dropping down small waterfalls and weaving your way through the rapids. If the thought of any of this scares you, just give it a try—it's the perfect opportunity to look fear in the eye and say, "Not today!" White-water rafting also strengthens your teamwork skills if you go with friends, family, or your partner.

## Take an Archery Class

The best activities are the ones that challenge you mentally and physically. Archery requires a combined focus of both mind and body as you aim your bow toward your target and release. Unlike other physically demanding activities, though, archery isn't all about a quick rush of adrenaline sparked by danger. It's thrilling because it demands patience, focus, and self-motivation to improve, and the rush you get is from hitting that target all by yourself. Archery also teaches a growth mindset—simply acting frustrated and flustered or quitting won't get you anywhere with the sport. It takes some serious determination to become a pro archer.

## Tell Your Boss Why You Deserve a Raise

Advocating for yourself can be nerve-racking, but when it comes to moving up the ladder at work, it's sometimes necessary. The key is having a clear understanding of what you deserve, how a raise would help not only you but the entire team, and a healthy dose of confidence. Entering the situation equipped and prepared with these three tools will ensure that the experience is less scary and more thrilling, no matter how it shakes out.

**BONUS TIP**

These negotiations shouldn't start at your annual review. Normalize regular communication with your manager about what you want out of your career. Set a follow-up at the end of a big project to discuss what you just accomplished and ask for honest feedback. It may get your heart pumping to initiate conversations like this, but take it as a sign that you're pushing yourself in the right direction!

## Learn How to Skateboard or Roller-Skate

Besides looking really cool zipping around town on a skateboard or on roller skates, skating is a good way to practice the act of getting back up again when you fall. The truth is that while learning how to skate, you will fall! That's totally okay, though, and all part of the process. Falling aside, there are tons of reasons why you should pick up skating as a hobby. All you need is one piece of equipment and some padding to get started. You can teach yourself (*YouTube* videos help), and it's good physical exercise. The

idea of messing up is scary, but once you get up and dust yourself off from your first spill, you'll be ready to hop back up for more thrills.

## Solve High-Stakes Puzzles with Friends

Have you ever had a nightmare in which you're trapped in a room with no way to escape? Claustrophobes, beware, for that's the whole premise of an escape room. It sounds awful, so exactly why have they become so popular? Because of the thrill factor! It's a scary situation, but you know that it's also a controlled one. It also helps that you'll never be alone, as many of them require at least two players to work together to solve the puzzles and escape the room. Most of the time, the point of an escape room is to exercise your teamwork skills to accept challenges, find clues, get into character, and come out victorious. It puts your brain to work in a fun way and can be done with friends, family, or even colleagues.

## Sign Up for an Open Mic

Whether or not you have a passion for singing, participating in an open mic night is a thrilling way to learn how to feel comfortable performing in front of an audience. If singing really isn't your thing, challenge yourself in other ways, like performing in a poetry slam or even an open mic stand-up comedy show. Shake off your nerves by bringing a friend who is also willing to perform, or, even better, you two can perform together. You'll have a great time if you just go for it and don't take yourself too seriously, and you'll create memories that you can look back on and laugh about in the future.

## Learn a Challenging New Skill

Believe it or not, continually learning new skills can literally change the way our brains work—which can be thrilling without being dangerous! If presented with a challenging situation, our body and minds adapt to deal with it—our muscles get stronger, and our brain connections become faster. The opposite happens when we're being couch potatoes for too long. When it comes to our brains, it's use it or lose it! Challenging yourself to be a lifelong learner doesn't just make things more fun; it actually improves your life in so many ways.

**BONUS TIP**

If you want to learn glass blowing or how to ride a motorcycle, go for it. If you've always wanted to try baking or knitting, also go for it. Much of our deepest satisfaction in life comes from a willingness to expose ourselves to new challenges, no matter what that means to you.

## Go Scuba Diving

For those attracted to the unknown, why not begin exploring the most mysterious part of the planet? Those who take up scuba diving are exposed to a whole new part of the world that most people don't have access to, experiencing a sense of weightlessness as they glide under the water. Just as each destination is unique on land, so is every underwater ecosystem. Diving in tropical waters, you can see a rainbow of corals and fish, while at other diving sites you could encounter kelp forests, sunken ships, or squadrons of manta rays by night. In order to start diving you'll need to take a course to become PADI-certified, which is also ideal for meeting new friends.

## Reinvent Your Wardrobe

If you look good, you feel good. And looking "good" means looking like your most authentic self. Throughout our lives, we're constantly evolving and changing, so why shouldn't our look follow suit? If you've been wearing clothes that don't accurately represent your personality and energy anymore, it can be thrilling to switch things up and surprise the people in your life with a reinvigorated new you. And it doesn't require a big budget, either.

### HOW IT WORKS

Go through your closet and create a donation pile of everything that no longer suits you. That donation pile can translate into key new pieces if you bring them into thrift stores that offer store credit, like Buffalo Exchange and Out of the Closet. When you're shopping for new clothes that really speak to you, focus on quality over quantity, picking a mix of dynamic items and those that let your personal style shine.

## Zip Around Town on a Moped

Believe it or not, you don't need to be located in charming Italy to get around town on a Vespa or moped. It's a fun, relatively safe way to travel locally, and it's becoming easier to do in most cities too. A happy medium between the breeziness of a bike and the excitement of a motorcycle, mopeds top out at about 40 miles per hour, making them ideal for zipping around your town or city. You can also rent a moped for the day for much less than a car, and you don't need a motorcycle license to ride one. Check where you live for ride-sharing options for mopeds, which makes this activity super affordable.

## Ask Someone on a Date

One challenge that's scarier than jumping out of a plane physically is doing so emotionally—asking someone out on a date. While you may dread it, it can really push you out of your comfort zone and lead to meeting someone special!

**HOW IT WORKS**

The first key in asking someone out is to accept that rejection is a natural part of life (and always a possibility). It's also important to make your intentions clear: Don't ask someone to "hang out"; ask if they'd like to go on a date. The next time you find yourself connecting with someone, take a look at the person's body language. Are they engaging with you and smiling, or crossing their arms and shifting in their seat? If it seems like you have the green light, then go for it! The worst that could happen is they say no, which isn't the end of the world. As they say, there are plenty of fish in the sea.

## Take an Improv Course

Here's one that will really keep you on your toes. Improv (short for *improvisation*) is a unique form of stand-up comedy in which individuals perform jokes and comical activities by bouncing off the other members of the improv group. Taking an improv class is a great way to get over your fears of making a fool out of yourself, because that's literally the objective of the class. Besides improving your public-speaking skills, you'll also learn how to actively listen as you join in on jokes being told by your classmates, and you will probably make friends in the process.

## Ask Someone You Admire to Be Your Mentor

Maybe you've been following someone on social media forever, or you've hungrily consumed all of their interviews by way of magazines and podcasts. Maybe it's someone at work whose career and work ethic you admire. Regardless of who this person is to you, you're impressed and maybe just a little intimidated by them. It makes sense that asking them to be your mentor would be nerve-racking! A supportive mentor can help give you unbiased advice, tips and secrets about your industry, connect you to like-minded people, and more. Start by reaching out with a thoughtful message giving clear reasons why you think you two would be a good mentor and mentee match, and pitch the idea of an initial conversation to see how you mesh. During the conversation, make sure to communicate what you expect from the relationship in terms of time commitment, and what kind of guidance you're seeking.

## Try Something Spicy with Your Partner

If things in your relationship have started to feel a bit beige lately, it may be time to take the initiative of adding a little bit of spice. Start with a few simple messages letting your partner know you're thinking about them—maybe texting them something flirty before they get home from work or tucking a handwritten note into their bag. When the time is right, ask them if there's something new they want to try—or share something that's been on your mind. You may be scared to share, but that's part of the thrill.

**BONUS TIP**

It may not sound very sexy, but if you're looking to get spicy in the bedroom more often, schedule regular times to be intimate. That's one calendar appointment you won't mind hearing an alert for.

## Try All the Foods You Hated As a Kid

Maybe you absolutely hated olives growing up or couldn't handle anything spicy, or the idea of raw fish made you cringe. Do you still live by those same outdated gastronomical principles, swearing off anything on a restaurant menu that includes culinary elements that you didn't enjoy while growing up? News flash: It's been decades, and palates change drastically! Next time it's your turn to choose a dinner spot with your partner or friends, surprise them by choosing a cuisine you'd typically steer away from. Go all in, trying everything unfamiliar—you never know what you may end up loving. Stepping outside of your comfort zone, regardless of whether you end up liking the food or not, will be thrilling for you and impressive to those you're sharing the meal with.

## Swing Through the Air on a Flying Trapeze

Sometimes it feels good to just let go, but in flying trapeze lessons it feels even better to grab back on again a few seconds later. Just like you may have seen at a circus performance before, the flying trapeze involves tall platforms with bars to swing from, leap off, and grab back on to. Flying trapeze stunts also involve swinging upside down and grabbing the hands of another performer. Though it sounds dangerous, it's actually not, as a cushy net sits below waiting to catch you if you fall. The possibility of falling, and of flying, is where the thrill lies. It's a great physical activity, a super fun date idea, and an exercise in trust.

## Take More Naps

Yes—you read that right. Numerous studies, including one conducted by NASA, have shown that short naps can increase your performance at work, make you smarter, improve your reaction time, and make you happier. The thrill of napping comes from its unfortunate taboo. In places like the United States and the United Kingdom, where the rat race reigns supreme, naps are traditionally seen as a lazy thing to do. You know better, though, which is why tomorrow afternoon you're going to take a twenty-minute, well-deserved afternoon snooze and feel great about it.

## Go Skinny-Dipping

The last time you went skinny-dipping may have been decades ago as a result of a triple dog dare, but I'm here to dare you to try it once again. Swimming in your birthday suit is a thrilling, freeing activity that shouldn't be age restrictive. Obviously, there is an appropriate time and place to skinny-dip—maybe you shouldn't go running into the ocean sans bathing suit in the middle of the afternoon (unless it's a nude beach, of course). Speaking of nude beaches, they are the perfect opportunity to unclothe without feeling too naughty. Everyone around you is experiencing the joy of feeling the wind where it usually doesn't blow, so why not join in on the fun?

## Add More Spontaneity to Your Life

Spontaneity is the spice of life, and a good dose of it may be just what you need to bring some fun back into your routine. There are simple ways to be spontaneous in your typical day, like actually stopping into that store or restaurant whose windows you always peer into as you pass by. Next time you're feeling low, treat yourself to a big scoop of ice cream or call a friend and ask them if you can come over, rather than planning to spend time together weeks down the line.

**BONUS TIP**

If you're ready for a true act of spontaneity, pack your bags for a weekend trip and book yourself a ticket on the next affordable flight out of town. It will feel exhilarating to make a spur-of-the-moment decision, and you'll be on your way to making memories you won't soon forget.

## Work on Becoming More Decisive

It's easy to get caught up in the minutiae of every decision you have to make, taking time to mull everything over until you're more confused than when you started. Instead, make a conscious effort to be more decisive, answering immediately with your gut instinct rather than constantly second-guessing yourself. Making more decisions this way won't just feel good—it'll signal to others that you're a confident person who knows what you want.

## Hit the Big Rides at an Amusement Park

When was the last time you visited an amusement park as an adult, with only adults in tow? If your answer is "I don't know," then maybe it's time to plan a trip. Amusement parks are an ideal place to tap back in to your inner child, joyfully eating junk food and semi-reluctantly facing your fear of heights on the roller coasters. That nostalgic feeling of childlike happiness is uniquely freeing, and coupled with the adrenaline rush of an intimidating ride, it makes for a perfect day. Just try to give yourself some time to digest that funnel cake before hopping on the next ride—your stomach will surely thank you for it.

## Smile at a Stranger

Making eye contact with strangers is usually awkward. It's even more so when the two of you pretend like it didn't even happen, casting your eyes down at the floor as fast as you are humanly able. Instead, next time you lock eyes with someone, simply tilt your head up and give them a warm smile. It doesn't need to insinuate anything—it can just be a friendly reminder of our shared humanity, and regardless of whether they smile back or not, you can feel assured that you came off as the friendly, confident one in the situation. It's a thrilling feeling.

## Head Out to a Party and Don't Watch the Clock

To set the scene: It's a Friday night, you're at your friend's place surrounded by people you enjoy, and you're thinking about work. Or what time you have to wake up the next morning. Or whatever else that little voice of anxiety is whispering into your ear. Well, it's time to finally break that toxic cycle! Next time you head out to a party or any other kind of social engagement, revel in the thrill of having a good time without clock watching or worrying.

**BONUS TIP**

Just as you might do while trying to meditate, don't block negative thoughts out completely. Acknowledge them as they come to you, and then release them to tackle at another time and place. It may be tough to do at first, but it will become second nature the more you mindfully practice the mental exercise.

## Add Elements of Adventure to Your Next Vacation

There's absolutely nothing wrong with lounging on the beach during vacation, and you deserve the relaxation time. Think about how amazing that time spent on the sand will feel, though, if it's juxtaposed with just a little bit of action and adventure. If that usually isn't your thing, then add just one exciting activity to the itinerary, like jet skiing, paragliding, a helicopter tour, a challenging hike—the list goes on. For those looking to really push themselves, lots of destinations are made for just that. One great option is Queenstown, New Zealand, widely considered to be the adventure capital of the world.

## Redecorate Your Space

Americans spend a lot of time in their homes. In fact, the Environmental Protection Agency (EPA) says we spend a whopping 93 percent of our life indoors. So how you decorate your nest has a huge impact on how you feel. While redecorating may not seem thrilling at first, it can be exciting to switch up the vibe in your space, no matter how small or large the change.

### HOW IT WORKS

Grab a printed layout of your space (or draw a rudimentary one yourself) and mark where the furniture is currently. Now switch it up, moving pieces around to better fit your everyday life. Finally, add a piece of artwork or a kitchen gadget that will make you happy to look at or to use, like a French press for your morning coffee or a funky ceramic vase that you want to fill with flowers.

## Take a Surfing Lesson

For all its beauty, the ocean can be scary, with its intense vastness and powerful waves. That's what makes surfing so exhilarating, though! When life gets overwhelming, picking one task and absolutely owning it can make you feel like you finally have things back under control. Surfing is a physical manifestation of this feeling, as you conquer the unwilling ocean one wave at a time. Just like any other difficult skill, you may not be an ace when you first hop on the board, but when you do finally ride out a wave, it will be all the more satisfying.

**BONUS TIP**

For safety reasons and to expedite your skill level, don't attempt to surf alone (or even with experienced surfer friends!) for your first time. Sign up for a multiday course if you're on vacation somewhere by the beach, or at least schedule an afternoon lesson with a certified instructor. You'll be glad you did.

## Mix Up Your Daily Routine

There is a lot of comfort in a good routine. Sometimes life can feel a little redundant, though, when you follow the same schedule every single weekday—especially if you aren't giving yourself enough time in the morning before work to really wake up, or before bed to relax and unwind. Mixing things up in your routine will not only help to continually improve it; it will also spark more joy and excitement in your day. Implement some simple shifts once per week, like waking up earlier and starting your day with something that makes you happy. During your lunch break, try a new spot and totally unplug from your email, adding a little bit of a thrill to your day.

# CHAPTER 9

# Stay Social
# While Solo Traveling

You've been begging your friends to finally take that group trip you've been discussing for years, but somehow nothing ever materializes. Maybe you can't agree on a destination, have conflicting schedules, or don't see eye to eye on a budget. Regardless of the reason why, the trip doesn't seem to be happening. Enter stage left: solo travel.

Every move you make while solo traveling is up to you. You can sleep in until noon if you want to and spend a whole day just wandering around, or change up your schedule on a whim. You can eat the same thing five days in a row, or take someone back to your hotel room. The world is your oyster!

This chapter is all about the art of solo traveling while remaining social. It's inevitable that you will get lonely from time to time if you're traveling solo. But there's a whole world of new friends to meet while you're out on your adventure, whether at a pub crawl in Amsterdam or while learning how to make Thai green curry in Chiang Mai.

## Stay at a Hostel

While traditionally unglamorous, hostels are perhaps the best way to meet people while traveling solo. Hostels are super communal in nature, so you may even be sharing a room with new friends, and if not you'll surely strike up a conversation in the lobby, the kitchen area, or at the bar. But you don't even have to stay at a hostel to make friends at one, as many have bar areas that are open to the public. For those looking to board for the night in a hostel, options have improved over the years, with hotel brands like Freehand and Generator elevating the idea of what a hostel can look and feel like.

## Enroll Yourself in a Cooking Class with Local Cuisine

You simply cannot go to Thailand without learning how to make green curry, or to Italy without hand shaping your own pasta. Besides coming home with new culinary knowledge to impress friends with, you'll meet other outgoing travelers who are also looking to learn new skills. Don't be afraid to strike up a conversation and ask your fellow amateur chefs what their plans are for the rest of their trips. Before you know it, you'll go from rolling out dough together to hitting the bars later that night.

## Keep Your Body Language Open

If your goal is to make friends, it's important to make a concerted effort to be open and friendly while traveling solo. Always be mindful of your surroundings, of course, and listen to your gut feeling if someone seems sketchy, but otherwise the best way to meet nice people while you're in a new environment is to exude a friendly, approachable vibe. In terms of body language, that means not constantly standing with your arms crossed and your eyes down, afraid to make eye contact. Don't be afraid to step up and initiate conversation, either! Showing a genuine, light-hearted interest in your fellow travelers is something that they'll most likely appreciate.

## Take a Guided Group Tour with Other Solo Travelers

Guided city tours let you hit all of your destination's highlights in a short amount of time while learning interesting stories and historical tidbits on the way. These fun and informative guided tours are often frequented by solo travelers, so they can be an easy way to meet other newcomers to the city. You'll be able to bond with a possible new friend over the beauty of the location and compare plans that you've made for the rest of your respective trips. If the two of you pass by a spot on the tour that you both want to explore more, try making plans for the next day to go check it out together!

## Stay in a Hotel in the Middle of the City

Hotels and rental properties that are removed from the city center can be perfect for a relaxed trip or solo respite, but they're not as ideal for meeting new people. Staying in a place located too far from the action means you'll likely need to tuck in earlier than you might if you were staying closer by, and it's likely that any new friends you make won't be staying anywhere close to your temporary abode. If you have plans to make connections while in town, try opting for a spot in the middle of the city, where you can wake up in the morning and instantly be a part of the infectious energy of the destination.

## Take Public Transportation

Traveling to a foreign place and then having to figure out how to get around is overwhelming. It can be tempting to cab everywhere and cut out public transportation, but that actually isn't a good idea for a few reasons. First, taking the bus or subway around town gives you a better sense of how the city is laid out. That will hopefully help you to understand the destination a little better, and that knowledge will be invaluable as you make spontaneous decisions for where to dine and what sights you plan to see. Most important, public transportation gives you an opportunity to meet fellow travelers and locals. If you feel unsure about which bus to hop on next, don't be afraid to strike up a conversation with someone who can point you in the right direction. You never know where a single conversation can lead!

## Seek Out Communal Dining Experiences

You'll find plenty of opportunities to dine with a group while traveling, even if you're coming solo. Before you even arrive at the destination, research dinner events, which usually seat people at long tables perfect for mingling, and you'll get to try some amazing food at them too. If you haven't booked anything prior to your arrival, seek out communal tables at bars, cafés, and restaurants, where it's almost more awkward if you don't strike up a conversation with the person sitting right next to you or across from you. Even if you're typically a shy person, remember that the people who sat down at the communal tables most likely did so with the same intentions as you.

## Tap In to Your Network

If you already have good friends who live at your travel destination, this is a no-brainer. Search through your friends list on social media and even on sites like *LinkedIn* for connections you may have there. It doesn't matter if it's been years since you've spoken to them—try reaching out! Even if they don't have time to show you around while you're there, at least they'll have tons of local insider knowledge to give you. You can also put out a widespread call on social media or by way of a group text or email to let your friends know where you're headed and ask them if they know anyone who lives in the area. You may be surprised by the responses you get!

## Check Out a Show or Cultural Event

Some of the most epic trips happen when you travel for an event or holiday synonymous with your destination, like Carnival in Brazil, Día de los Muertos in Mexico, or Midsummer in Sweden. But there are lots of other ways to expose yourself to a destination's unique culture while also meeting fun new people by attending shows, festivals, and other social events.

**BONUS TIP**

Many of these events are fun because of the large crowds they attract, but that also means you should stay alert and aware of your person and belongings at all times. If you plan on bringing a bag with you, find one that straps closely onto your body with a zipper or button closure.

## Join a Solo Traveler *Facebook* Group

If you've never solo traveled before or you're considering a destination and want to gauge important factors like safety level and price, an online solo traveler group is an invaluable resource. In the group, you'll find everything from personal stories to destination guides and more. It's also the perfect place to announce to a new group of like-minded people that you're about to head out on a solo trip, and to see if anyone will be around for a coffee, drink, or other adventure. If you're already at your destination and have a question or find yourself in a sticky situation, the group can act as an informed sounding board.

## Attend Language Exchanges

Most people learn a language best by way of cultural immersion. If you're staying at a certain destination for a few weeks, language exchanges can be a powerful tool to help you learn a language quickly, make new connections, and teach someone else your own language as well.

### HOW IT WORKS

Check social media sites, travel forums, and bulletin boards at local coffee shops, or with your host family (if you're staying with one) for language exchange meetups in the area. Once you arrive, you'll find someone to partner with, and you can both use the time to improve your respective foreign language skills. Half the time will be spent on one language and the other half on the other language. Not only is this a great way to learn, but the whole point of it is to talk to people, meaning there's a chance you'll make some awesome new connections.

## Sign Up for a "Voluntourism" Experience

These volunteering-plus-tourism experiences allow you to travel for cheap while also doing good in the world as you volunteer your time for a good cause. They're cheap because you're typically able to swap your voluntary labor for free housing, and sometimes meals too. Some forms of voluntourism have gotten backlash for good reason, though, like working with children in Africa, which many deem as exploitative. Make sure to do your own thorough research before you sign up for one. There are still plenty of helpful ways you can donate your time while traveling. Another popular thing to do is volunteer at a hostel or bed and breakfast, which allows you to meet other travelers every day.

## Check Out *Reddit* Community Boards

If you've never utilized *Reddit* for travel tips, then you're missing out on a treasure trove of information! *Reddit* has some of the Internet's largest communities for everything you could think of. A great place to start is the subreddit /r/solotravel (the tagline reads "Where traveling solo is traveling social!"). Always super active thanks to its one million–plus members, this community is a must-join prior to your trip. Find conversation threads on anything from discussions on traveling as a woman over forty or as a person of color to road trip itineraries, safety tips, suggestions for working remotely, and more.

**BONUS TIP**

Once you've begun to interact with the community, post your own thread asking for any destination-specific advice you might be needing. You may find that other group members will be there at the same time, and you can schedule a meetup or compare itineraries.

## Embark On a Singles' Holiday

No travel partner, no problem. Seek out companies and resorts that offer singles-only travel—an ideal way to explore the world with other outgoing individuals. A quick Internet search will yield options for singles' trips that will have you zipping around Europe, seeking thrills in South America, or relaxing on a beach in the Caribbean with your new group of friends. There are also hotels and resorts around the world, especially all-inclusive ones, which have amazing solo traveler offers. Some of these resorts, like BodyHoliday on the island of Saint Lucia, even offer one month out of each year devoted solely to those flying solo.

## Sign Up for a Pub Crawl

The idea of a pub crawl might have you saying, "That would have been fun [insert however many] years ago," but don't knock it until you try it. While out at the pubs in lively cities like Dublin, Berlin, and Amsterdam, you're bound to meet travelers of all ages from around the world who are all there to have a social, fun time. You can sign up for an organized pub crawl online before your trip, which ensures that you have a built-in group to bop from bar to bar with. You're bound to chat with the people in your group, and as soon as many of the pub goers hear your foreign accent, you'll have people asking where you're from—an easy icebreaker. If you're not in a place where pub crawls are a thing, search out something comparable, like a salsa evening in Cuba.

## Post Up at a Charming Sidewalk Café

If you're spending multiple days in one location, it can feel like the ultimate treat to give yourself a day of rest and relaxation in between an otherwise nonstop itinerary of sightseeing and adventure. Instead of spending all day at your hotel, though, bring some reading material along for an afternoon spent lingering at a charming local café. If you can, nab a spot outside or in a communal area, where you'll have the best people-watching opportunities and a chance to converse with locals and fellow travelers. Just make sure that you're not loitering for too long without ordering anything; this gives you a great excuse to keep your cup of coffee full and to try a few different things on the menu.

## Bond over Photography

When you're traveling solo, you may have an even stronger than usual desire to capture some amazing images from your trip so that you can share them with loved ones when you return. A love of photography is nearly universal among avid travelers, which means there are tons of other travelers who want to take photos together. Consider looking into a photo walk, which is an organized group activity where you simply walk around with a group of other amateur (and sometimes professional!) photographers, snapping images and comparing them with one another.

**BONUS TIP**

If you'd like one of your fellow travelers to take some photos of you, try offering to take one of them first. Demonstrate that you're making a concerted effort to get a great shot of them, testing out different angles and poses. When it comes time for them to ask if you'd like one, too, they'll already know which angles you prefer when it comes to portraits.

## Take a Dance Class

Learn some new moves to take out onto the club floor at a local dance class. Not only is learning some regional dance steps a culturally rich activity; it's also a great workout and the perfect opportunity to make some new friends in a no-pressure environment. Everyone who signed up for the class is likely a novice dancer, so you'll all start out on an even playing field and will get to laugh together as you attempt to master the moves. Once you've got some of them down, look out for any local bars and lounges in the area that are planning dance nights for while you're still in town.

## Find Your Zen (and New Friends) at a Wellness Retreat

We all experience burnout once in a while. Solo traveling can be an amazing respite from the hustle and bustle of everyday life, and even more so when you're planning to attend a wellness retreat. While yoga retreats typically get all the attention, a wellness retreat can consist of many variations. Retreats can be focused on healthy eating, mindful adventure activities, farming, breath work, and more. Regardless of your interests, there's likely a retreat available to help you recharge your internal batteries. While there, you're guaranteed to meet other participants who you'll be able to spend time with, share stories with, and relate to on multiple levels.

## Sign Up for a Group Trip

If you don't feel comfortable jetting off to a new country alone, an organized group trip is a great option. Group trips are almost exclusively booked by solo travelers, and lots of companies offer them with destinations all around the globe. Group trips help take the guesswork out of traveling, too, as a full itinerary of activities is already arranged for you. Many group trips require you to submit an application with a bit about yourself, so you can be assured that the guides putting the trips together are being mindful about which travelers will mesh well together. These kinds of trips provide easy options for making friends, rather than having to rely on staying in hostels or making conversation with strangers while you're already on your trip. Exodus, Contiki, and Intrepid are well-known companies that organize trips around the world, but don't count out smaller organizers as well, which you can find and read reviews about online.

## Eat Your Meals at the Bar

When you're a solo traveler, every meal is a possible opportunity to strike up conversation and make connections. One of the best places to do that is at the bar, which solo diners tend to frequent. Sitting at a normal table is nice, too, if you just feel like posting up with a book for some quiet time and to enjoy your meal, but you're not likely to meet anyone while sitting at your own table in a restaurant. Instead, seek out communal spaces like the bar and chat up the bartender or whoever is sitting next to you if they seem friendly and open to conversation. You're likely to hear some interesting stories from people sitting at the bar, whether you make friendships with those you meet or not.

## Stay with a Local Host

Want to meet the locals? Stay in their house! If you book your stay on Airbnb, you'll be staying in someone's home, giving you a unique peek into how people live their lives in your destination city. While looking on the site, make sure to look at options that provide you either with a shared or private room rather than the entire property, which would mean that you're staying there alone. Airbnb has options that range from fancy to affordable, making it easy to find the right accommodation for you. Another option would be to check out Couchsurfing, where you can write a bio to tell travelers a bit about yourself. People use the popular app to find free accommodations and also to meet up with other community members.

## Use a Solo Traveler App

Check out the many apps worth downloading before you head out on a solo trip. Each is designed to make your experience more seamless. Some travel apps specialize in ways to keep you safe, some include handy trip-planning functionality, and others are great for meeting new people abroad. One unique app that's great for the gastronomically obsessed is called Eatwith, which brings strangers together over a meal. Use it to check out local dinner parties, food tours, cooking lessons, and more while you're traveling. You're bound to meet lots of people and make some delicious memories along the way.

## Pick a Solo-Friendly Destination

While there are amazing things to experience in each country, some destinations naturally lend themselves to being more solo traveler–friendly. Depending on the kind of activities you're planning, top destinations can vary widely, but the number one consideration for any solo traveler should be safety. If you're not an experienced solo traveler, do your own ample research before picking somewhere known for a low crime rate and high quality-of-life index. For adventure seekers looking to have thrilling experiences, that may mean a trip to Iceland, New Zealand, or Santiago. Those looking for an amazing food scene and vibrant cities should perhaps consider places like Spain, Japan, or Vietnam.

## Sign Up for a Day-Long Excursion

Guided day tours are an awesome way to access immersive experiences outside of a city without having to rent a car or figure out complicated logistics on your own. For example, a day tour leaving from San Juan in Puerto Rico might involve a day of tromping through the rainforest to a waterfall or boating around to different islands to access amazing snorkeling locations. These tours involve a guide or two and a small group of travelers, many of whom are usually traveling solo or with just one other friend. Regardless of the activity, you're locked in to spend all day long with the group, meaning it's inevitable that you'll find at least one person that you end up bonding with.

## Learn Some of the Language Beforehand

If you're traveling to a country where English isn't widely spoken (or spoken at all), you'll do yourself a world of good by learning at least a few key words and phrases before your trip. Travelers shouldn't assume that everyone on their travels will speak English, and it will delight most of the people you come across that you took the time to learn a bit of their language. One of the easiest ways to learn is by downloading a free language-learning app like Duolingo. There are also tons of *YouTube* videos and podcasts that specifically tackle phrases you will need during your trip, like finding the bathroom, asking for a price, and saying please and thank you.

**BONUS TIP**

If you don't have time to learn any of the destination language prior to your trip, download an app like Hello Talk, which utilizes Google Cloud translation capabilities to translate in real time for free.

## Approach Groups Traveling Together

It can be tempting to avoid groups as someone flying solo, but try not to be intimidated. Most of the time, groups of friends are just as happy to make new connections as those who are traveling solo. Whether you meet a friend duo or a larger group on tours, at bars and lounges, or during a class, it doesn't hurt to at least make conversation. Chances are they'll love that you're interacting with them, and if all goes well, you'll be making more than one new friend at a time.

## Stay in One Place for At Least a Week

It's easy to travel around in a place like Europe and be tempted to stay at each destination for only a couple of days—there's so much to see! The problem with hopping from one city to the next so quickly is that you won't have the time to get any sense of what it's actually like to live there beyond the major highlights and tourist attractions. You also won't have as much time to make connections with fellow travelers.

**BONUS TIP**

If possible, try to stay in at least one of the cities you're visiting for at least a week, which will allow you to take your time each day rather than rushing around, trying to see everything before you jet off again.

## Tap In to Your Favorite Hobbies

When you're traveling around an unfamiliar destination, it can feel comforting to tap in to hobbies you regularly turn to while you're back at home. Those hobbies can also present ways to connect with locals, expats, and other travelers who also enjoy them. For example, just because you're on a trip in Australia doesn't mean you can't meet up with a group of locals to knit together. Log in to sites like *Meetup* that will help you find community from pretty much anywhere.

## Apply for Remote Year

If you don't have to work in an office onsite to get your job done, you can apply for an epic solo travel adventure through Remote Year. If accepted into one of their programs, you'll work remotely while traveling around the world for an entire year, spending each month in a new city. Each program is made up of handpicked individuals from all over the world, so you'll get to spend a whole year getting to know a new group of friends that you'll make memories with in a plethora of destinations. It's an ideal situation for solo travel enthusiasts because you won't even need to take time off from work in order to be traveling for 365 days.

## Try Train Travel

If you've never experienced a multicity train journey before, now is your time! Plenty of destinations lend themselves well to being explored by train, from Japan to Canada to Switzerland. Each one has something different to offer, of course, but the point is to be able to take in the sights while zooming through different landscapes, hopping off as you wish for afternoons spent wandering around different cities and points of interest. When traveling by train, strike up a conversation with your seatmate or those sitting near you. If you two don't end up vibing, you can just sit by someone new when you get back on.

## Find the Local Hangouts

Every city has those couple of spots that are always bustling with people, or certain areas that get super busy during a certain part of the day. Consult forums, social media, and friends who have traveled to your destination before so you can nail down the location of these special spots. Maybe it's a park or beach that really picks up after the workday is over, or an outdoor beer garden that everyone brings their dogs to. Regardless, these are places not to be missed: They exude a certain kind of unique energy found nowhere else, and they're the best places to meet possible new connections!

## Reach Out to Expats

An expat (an abbreviated form of the word *expatriate*) refers to someone who is living outside their home country. No matter where you spin a globe and point, you'll surely find an expat community there. Finding expats to connect with will help you in a number of ways. They'll most likely be happy to give you suggestions on how to stay safe and have the best time while visiting their new country of residence, and they may even offer to show you around town or provide you with a place to stay. It's most helpful when you can find an expat to connect with who shares your unique situation when it comes to travel—for example, if you're a woman traveling alone or a member of the LGBTQ+ community. There are lots of ways to seek out expat communities, but one of the easier ones is through social media groups and online forum sites such as *Reddit*.

## Bring a Deck of Cards

You never know where you might be when someone strikes up a conversation unexpectedly. If you'd love to keep chatting, a great ice-breaker is a simple deck of cards, which can fit easily in your pants pocket or a small purse. Bring it with you to a hotel lounge, the common area of a hostel, the communal tables at a café, or anywhere else that people tend to congregate. Watch how quickly you'll end up in a game of gin rummy with a new group of friends. There's nothing like a bit of competition to facilitate bonding and joking.

# CHAPTER 10

# Take a
## Bucket List Trip

Everyone has a bucket list, whether it's cataloged in writing or simply stored away in your head. Rarely do we check off those items, though, and that's a shame. One of the major themes in this book is that in order to grow and live our best lives, we have to challenge ourselves to step outside of our comfort zones, to make connections, and to rethink what we once thought was improbable.

The point of a bucket list is to have amazing, incredible things to look forward to, and that doesn't matter if you're not actually working your way through it. Now is the time to take that first bucket list trip, and that's what this chapter is all about: giving you the inspiration to decide which experiences are right for you.

While you're going through the list, pay attention to the keywords that make your ears perk up or your eyes brighten. Think critically about why those experiences might be the most life-changing for you, whether that sets you on a path to Iceland to see the northern lights, to the night markets of Vietnam, or on a sailboat riding the waves off the coast of Maine.

## Release Baby Turtles Into the Ocean in Costa Rica

If you've ever seen an episode of *Planet Earth*, you probably already know that sea turtles take on a harrowing journey as soon as they hatch from their eggs. As they make their way as quickly as possible from the sand into the ocean, many of them get snapped up by hungry seabirds. In fact, only one in about a thousand makes it to adulthood, and all seven species of sea turtles are considered endangered. Fortunately, there are hatcheries in places like Mexico and Costa Rica where you can sign up to help conservationists safely escort newly hatched baby turtles on their journey to the water. Helping such delicate little beings confidently waddle away from the comfort of their eggs is a moving experience, and a bonding one for you and whoever you make the journey with.

## Take a Pasta-Making Class in Italy

A trip to anywhere in Italy pretty much ensures you'll be eating your fair share of delicious, fresh pasta. You may not know, though, that each region of Italy is known for different pasta shapes and styles. Farfalle (also known as bow-tie pasta) is the signature pasta of the northwestern region of Lombardy, while Puglia to the southeast is famous for orecchiette. With all this pasta knowledge at your fingertips, you'd be remiss not to take a class where you can learn from locals how to make it yourself. Cooking classes abroad are always a fun way to meet and bond with other travelers, and you'll get to show off your pasta-making skills to friends back home too.

## Go to the Filming Site of Your Favorite Epic Movie

Taking a trip to the filming site of a classic movie can feel surreal in the most epic way. On tours of these locations, you're almost guaranteed to be shoulder to shoulder with other fans of the film or franchise, creating an exciting collective energy that you'll always remember. And many film locations are stunning in their own right, like the country of New Zealand, where the Lord of the Rings trilogy was filmed. One of the most popular stops on the Lord of the Rings tour is the picturesque village of the Shire, with its round wooden doors that lead into the hillsides. Meanwhile, Harry Potter fans can visit Oxford's Christ Church Cathedral, which stood in as Hogwarts School of Witchcraft and Wizardry in the films. The cathedral offers a walking tour. On the Hawaiian island of Kauai, you can find Jurassic Park buffs touring the filming locations, most of which are only accessible by guided tour.

## Travel to Iceland to See the Northern Lights

Chances are you've seen plenty of photos of the northern lights (the aurora borealis) as it flashes otherworldly colors of green, purple, and pink across the night sky. This unique natural phenomenon can only be seen from a small handful of locations in the world, and Iceland is one of the most popular. A trip to Iceland is epic in its own right, as you hike to the top of waterfalls, trek across glaciers, and meet other outgoing, adventurous travelers. The best time of year to see the northern lights is on crisp, cloudless winter nights, but their appearance is never guaranteed. Northern lights sightseeing tours are offered around the country by experts who eliminate as much of the guesswork as possible, so whether you're traveling alone or with a companion, you'll have a guide to an unforgettable experience.

## Meet Other Hikers at the Top of a Mountain Peak

There's something intrinsically connecting about reaching the peak of a challenging hike and finding others there who have also completed the climb. Your hiking bucket list is sure to be unique, since everyone has different heights they want to reach. Some may aspire to climb Mount Everest, while others would be psyched to reach the top of Mount Rainier in Washington State.

**BONUS TIP**

Don't feel like your mountaineering bucket list has to match anyone else's; the sense of accomplishment you feel at the top is yours alone to enjoy. If the peaks you have on your list are amazing for beginners and moderate hikers, you'll probably want to add more challenging ascents once your first set have been conquered.

## Tour the Vineyards of Napa Valley

Known for its abundance of gorgeous vineyards, Napa Valley is a wine lover's paradise and the perfect location for a relaxing getaway with friends. This sprawling, picturesque, hilly region is magical to drive through, especially at golden hour, when the grass and grape leaves are illuminated with gold. Come with your closest friends to experience world-class wineries, Michelin-starred restaurants, pampering spa treatments, and an all-around luxurious time. Napa is also known as one of the top locations to ride a hot-air balloon, which is a bucket list item in itself.

## Plan an Ancestral Trip with Your Family

If you're one of the over thirty million people who have taken a DNA test to understand more about their heritage and genealogy, an ancestral trip might be one to tick off your bucket list soon. As it's a trip centered on exploring your family's homeland, it's only natural that at least some of your family members would hope to come along for the ride.

 **HOW IT WORKS**

The first step in planning an ancestral trip is to figure out whether you have enough knowledge to plan it on your own, or if you should hire a specialist. Start by asking your family what they know about your homeland, and if they know of any relatives who still live there. If you do have relatives there, you may not need any outside help, but if minimal information is known, hiring an expert can help facilitate connections and unlock meaningful experiences for you and your family.

## Spend a Wild Weekend in New York City

New York is one of the most visited cities in the world for a reason. It's a place with rich history—once the capital of the United States—and home to culturally significant monuments like the Statue of Liberty on Ellis Island. Lady Liberty was once an important homing beacon for immigrants from all over the world. Countless other attractions make New York worthy of your bucket list, from world-class museums to the internationally known Central Park. Many people also come to New York for its nightlife, which ranges from gritty dive bars to swanky, exclusive clubs, hidden speakeasies, and everything in between. The craziest night to be in New York, though, may be New Year's Eve, when people from all over the world come to see the ball drop in Times Square.

## Hit the Beach in Los Cabos, Mexico

A world-class beach destination, Los Cabos is split into two very different neighborhoods: Cabo San Lucas and San José del Cabo, connected by a long stretch of highway called the Corridor.

### HOW IT WORKS

Bring your most spontaneous friends for an unforgettable trip to Los Cabos that starts in Cabo San Lucas to the south—known best for its infamous nightlife, beach bars, and deluxe resorts. Once you're all tired of cradling hangovers from raucous nights, dig into some of the beautiful nature and authentic culture in the area, like at the iconic El Arco at the southernmost tip of Mexico. Accessible only by boat, it features a magnificent stone arch rising up from the waves. To the north, find officially designated magical towns like Todos Santos, small but mighty hubs for historical Mexican culture and sustainable farming experiences.

## Experience Mardi Gras in New Orleans

One of just a few unique festivals known by people around the world, Mardi Gras is often dubbed the "Greatest Free Show on Earth." A tradition that dates back thousands of years to pagan celebrations of spring, Mardi Gras is marked by several parades that make their way around town, leading up to the main event on the Tuesday before Lent begins. During this festival, New Orleans is one of the most joyous places on earth, with everyone from tourists to locals out on the street drinking hurricanes (the signature frozen beverage), throwing beaded necklaces, and dancing and singing to music. This is the kind of thing that you can let your figurative hair down for and be whoever and however you feel like being!

## Go Sailing in Maine

Maine is a ruggedly gorgeous New England state with an ample coastline waiting to be explored. An amazing trip to take solo or with one adventurous companion, a multiday sail off the coast of Maine is the ultimate nautical bucket list trip. If you've never sailed a day in your life, don't worry about it, because the best way to experience such a voyage is hopping aboard someone else's ship. Not only will you be in the good company of other travelers to befriend, but you also won't need to worry about the logistics of meals or even your itinerary. The tides themselves are unpredictable, making this trip the height of adventure travel, because you just have to go with the flow. You'll be rewarded with views of the sunrise and sunset over the water, and ample chances to paddleboard, swim, dine, and laugh with new friends.

## Learn How to Haggle in the Souks of Marrakech

The culturally rich city of Marrakech, Morocco, is probably on many bucket lists, and with good reason. The accommodations are world-class—do your visit to Marrakech right by splurging on a stay in a traditional riad. A riad, from the Arabic word for "garden," is a unique experience thanks to its defining inner courtyard. The real draw of the destination, though, is to wander the sand-colored walls of the medina in old Marrakech and experience the beautiful mayhem of everyday life there. As you make your way through the narrow mazes of the medina, resurface occasionally at one of the world-famous souks, or markets.

**BONUS TIP**

When it comes to securing the best prices, bring only small bills to the market, as larger bills will signal to sellers that you have a lot to spend. Start haggling at one-quarter of the displayed price, and never pay more than a third if you can help it.

## Cruise along the Coast of Alaska

Unlike a Caribbean cruise, a trip that travels around the rugged coast of Alaska manages to combine the best of both worlds—world-class luxury, ample chances to kick back and relax, and adventurous activities like dog sledding and kayaking by glaciers. Hop on an Alaskan cruise for a romantic vacation with your partner or bring the whole family. Cruises are also physically inclusive, so if you or your loved one isn't usually able to partake in adventurous journeys because of certain limitations, they'll be able to hop on board with you and spot bald eagles, seals, and whales, and relax with a book with a view of spectacular icy glaciers.

## Take a Bullet Train Across Japan

The best way to make your way around Japan is arguably by bullet train—a speedy and efficient representation of Japan's unique modernity. The bullet train is known for always being right on time. It's extremely clean and comfortable and travels at breakneck speeds of 200 miles per hour. While you're expected to maintain a respectful level of noise while on board, it's still likely that you could meet a fellow traveler and strike up a conversation while you whip past gorgeous scenery. Hopping on a bullet train, you'll snake your way across Japan's largest island, Honshu, starting in the exciting capital city of Tokyo. Just a few hours away is the calming port city of Kanazawa, full of renowned gardens, and from there you can travel another few hours to the cultural hub of Kyoto.

## Make New Friends in an Irish Pub

Ireland, otherwise referred to as the Emerald Isle, is known for its stunningly green landscape; its funny, friendly people; Guinness beer; and, of course, the classic Irish pub. The Irish pub has been re-created in cities around the world for its divelike approachability, warmth, and universal nostalgia. Traveling to Dublin, you'll see why Irish pubs became so popular in the first place and meet plenty of amazing people along the way.

**BONUS TIP**

If you're traveling alone or don't feel like doing research on the hundreds of different pubs around Dublin, the best thing you can do is sign up for a pub crawl. Your host, who will hopefully set the energy for the night, will know how to nab the best drink deals and where the choicest spots are in town. Just make sure to drink plenty of water!

## Hike Your Way to Machu Picchu

A trip to Machu Picchu is the dream of any adventure seeker or history buff, and if you consider yourself to be both, you should probably add the destination to your bucket list right now. Tucked away in the rugged Andes Mountains, the ancient city remained untouched until it was rediscovered in 1911.

**HOW IT WORKS**

If you are physically able and not afraid of a real challenge, the only way you should consider getting to Machu Picchu is by way of the Inca Trail. Believe it or not, the four-day journey is actually only a small part of the sprawling network of trails built by the Incas. A lot of the hike is directly uphill, too, but your reward at the end will be well worth the effort.

## Clink Steins at Oktoberfest in Germany

The famed Munich Oktoberfest is the biggest party in the world, and it has been celebrated for over two hundred years. Suffice to say, Oktoberfest is a once-in-a-lifetime opportunity to celebrate on an enormous scale with friends both old and new. The festival is about so much more than just drinking beer, too, with plenty to see and do. The event always begins with a citywide parade and a symbolic transport of beer kegs, one of which the mayor taps to proclaim the opening of Oktoberfest. Munich citizens of all ages take part in the festivities (yes, including kids!). That's because the more than 100 acres of festival grounds include everything from food and drink to rides, games, and live performances. All of this and the unmatched energy of the event make Oktoberfest more than bucket list–worthy, especially when you get to don the traditional dirndl or lederhosen.

## Discover the Natural Magic of a Bioluminescent Bay

Have you ever seen water sparkle at night? If you're spotting it in a Puerto Rico bay, that's not your eyes playing tricks on you—those are bioluminescent, single-celled organisms called dinoflagellates, whose bodies literally glow when triggered by touch and movement. There are only five bioluminescent bays in the entire world, and Puerto Rico is home to two of them. Considered to be the best and brightest in the world is Mosquito Bay on the small island of Vieques, where you can join a group of fellow nature lovers and a guide for an unforgettable time paddling around and experiencing the ocean glow.

## Go on a Safari in Tanzania

Speaking of animal lovers, it's impossible to talk about bucket list travel without mentioning a Tanzanian safari. One of the best places in the world to view the circle of life, a visit to Serengeti National Park is the ultimate in adventure travel and teaches you to expect the unexpected. Booking a safari with friends will deliver your group nonstop once-in-a-lifetime views: lions traipsing around with their cubs, wildebeests crossing the river, and giraffes reaching their long necks into the trees. At night you'll sit together by the campfire and literally sleep under the stars while the soundtrack of nature plays in the background.

## Learn How Tequila Is Made in Jalisco

The magic behind every sip of tequila you've ever had can be found in Jalisco, Mexico, where the agave spirit has an appellation of origin—meaning it can only legally be called tequila if it was produced there. Nestled deep within the region is the community for which the spirit is named, where you can have a bucket list experience driving past miles of blue agave fields and take a peek behind the scenes of the distilleries. For the most magical entrance, fly into Guadalajara—Mexico's second-largest city and worth its own trip. On weekends, you can even get there by way of a vintage-style black and gold train called the Jose Cuervo Express. Once you arrive, take your time touring the different distilleries and figuring out your own personal favorites.

## Pull an All-Nighter in Ibiza

The island of Ibiza, Spain, gets all the glory for being a world-class destination to party—and it should! Regardless of when you go for a visit, there's always something happening. Pool parties are on every day at O Beach, and by sunset, DJs are livening up the vibe on the most popular beaches with music, dancing, and live performances.

Once you've had enough, you can escape the eternal party by running off with your friends to explore hidden beaches, the ancient underground Can Marca Caves, or one of the island's many wineries.

## Swim with Whale Sharks in Mexico

Despite their misleading name, whale sharks aren't actually sharks at all. They're the world's largest species of fish, growing up to 60 feet in length, and totally safe to swim with. Floating underwater next to creatures that are so massive and beautiful is the ultimate bucket list adventure.

**HOW IT WORKS**

These gentle giants can be found swimming off the coast of Cancún, Mexico, from May to September. You'll have the best chance of seeing them in July and August. A guide will bring you and a small group out to the water in a boat, explaining more about whale sharks and how to swim near them without harming them. Once it's your turn to jump in, you must swim as fast as you can to catch up to the huge fish.

## Get Colorful at Holi in India

The Festival of Colors, or Holi, is a joyous annual celebration in India to mark the end of winter and imminent entrance of spring. Though it's now observed around the world, there's something very special about experiencing it where it originated. The night before Holi in India, bonfires are lit to celebrate the burning of Holika, an evil figure in Hinduism. For the two days that follow, colored powder is exuberantly tossed around, each color representing its own unique symbolism. Water-filled balloons and squirt guns add to the fun of this experience.

## Experience the Cherry Blossom Festival in Washington, DC

Nothing signals the start of spring like over three thousand Japanese cherry trees bursting with pink blossoms. They're all over the United States capital district of Washington, DC, concentrated around a small body of water called the Tidal Basin, which you can walk around while admiring the colorful blooms. Many impressive monuments, such as the Jefferson Memorial, the Lincoln Memorial, and the Washington Monument, are also nearby.

**BONUS TIP**

A trip to see the cherry blossoms is a beautiful bucket list trip for the whole family, but needs to be timed just right. The blossoms are fickle and only bloom for a few weeks out of the year, usually in late March or early April, so keep an eye out for bloom predictions before booking your flight.

## Wander the Christmas Market in Estonia

A walk through the Tallinn Christmas Market in Estonia is like something out of a storybook: powdery snow falling over glowing stalls in the historic Town Hall Square with pastel-colored buildings in the background framing the whole picture. Whether or not you observe the holiday, a trip to the market is worth it if only for the magical ambiance complete with twinkling lights, singing carolers, and mulled wine and chestnuts to warm yourself up with. The city itself has a long and interesting history, too, and the medieval city center of Tallinn is even designated as a UNESCO World Heritage Site.

## Watch the Sunset in Santorini

The crescent-shaped island of Santorini, Greece, is known for its iconic, whitewashed buildings perched precariously on cliffs above the sea. In the middle of the crescent lies Santorini's caldera—a depression caused by one of the most lethal earthquakes in history, which gave the island its unique shape. Besides exploring gorgeous beaches, eating fresh seafood, and visiting wineries, one of the most bucket list–worthy activities in Santorini is the simplest: watching the sunset. Arguably the best spot to watch is from the coastal town of Oia, which provides an incredible vantage point for watching the sun sink below the horizon line.

## Walk Through the Madness of Tokyo's Shibuya Crossing

An iconic representation of busy Tokyo, Shibuya Crossing is one of the most trafficked thoroughfares in the world, with over two thousand people crossing it at any one time. Sitting at the intersection of so many bus and train lines, Shibuya Crossing is literally the connection point of the city. It's also known for having an amazing nightlife and food scene. A trip here warrants donning your best outfits and showing off your unique style, as Shibuya is also known as a hub for young and fashionable locals.

**BONUS TIP**

Keep an eye out for the bronze statue of famous dog Hachikō at Exit 8 of Shibuya Station. Hachikō, who lived during the 1920s, patiently waited each day at Shibuya Station for his owner, a professor, to return home from his lectures. The ritual ended when the professor died suddenly without a chance to say goodbye to his beloved pet.

## Take a Hot-Air Balloon Ride over Cappadocia

The otherworldly landscape of Cappadocia, Turkey, is continually voted the best in the world for hot-air balloon rides, and iconic photos of the vessels taking to the air at sunrise are constantly flooding social media. Experience the once-in-a-lifetime adventure for yourself with a trip there.

### HOW IT WORKS

No matter when you decide to visit Cappadocia, you'll most likely be able to take a hot-air balloon ride, since it's one of the only locations in the world that offers them all year round. Once you book, be ready to wake up early, as the first hour of daylight is the safest time for ballooning. You'll be picked up before dawn and given breakfast while everything is organized, then ascend up to 3,000 feet in the air to see stunning valleys, unique rock formations, and ancient cave towns.

## Float Weightlessly in the Dead Sea

Israel's Dead Sea is at the top of a lot of people's bucket lists, partially because of its mind-boggling superlatives. Floating on its surface is easy because it's one of the saltiest bodies of water in the world, and at 1,300 feet below sea level, it's also the lowest point on earth. Come for a dip in the Dead Sea (which is actually a lake), not only for its turquoise-blue waters but also for its skin-healing properties. The mineral-rich water and black mud can supposedly help cure anything from eczema to cellulite and aging.

## Explore the Night Markets of Phu Quoc

Phu Quoc is a beautiful, serene island in the south of Vietnam. It's best known for its enormous national park full of lush jungle and sandy, white beaches, as well as its bustling night market. There, dozens of stalls sell authentic Vietnamese street food with a strong emphasis on seafood. For food lovers with a wide-ranging palate, this trip is a must, and it's made only more amazing by the other cool island features like the Hon Thom Cable Car, which you can ride for a full bird's-eye view of the stunning island.

## Participate in Thailand's Yi Peng Lantern Festival

When the full moon is reached on the twelfth month of the Thai lunar calendar (November), the northern city of Chiang Mai celebrates the Yi Peng Lantern Festival by releasing thousands of lanterns to float in the air and glide down the Ping River. Starting at sunset, groups line up in traditional costume to entertain festival goers, and students light lanterns and pass out candles along the waterfront.

 **BONUS TIP**

If you'd like to participate, you can book tickets for the largest lantern release at Maejo University, or buy your own flying paper lanterns from street vendors if you want to do it by yourself. When you release your lantern, it is customary to make a wish for the new year and put the past behind you.

## Take a Ride on the London Eye

An iconic, towering Ferris wheel situated on the South Bank of the River Thames, the London Eye is named for the panoramic views of the city it gives to anyone who rides it. On a clear day, it's possible to see up to 25 miles of London in all directions. While the London Eye is certainly a very touristy activity, it's worth it for the stunning views, and, if it's your first time in the city, seeing it in its entirety from up above gives you a better sense of how it's all laid out. If you don't want to wait in the mega-long line, make sure to book in advance and choose a Fast Track ticket option, which will be totally worth it when you don't have to spend half your afternoon waiting!

## Visit Sweden During Midsummer

While the Midsummer celebration in Sweden has religious origins, most Swedes today just love it because it celebrates the beautiful season of summer. Midsummer Eve is observed on the longest day of the year thanks to the summer solstice. A visit to the picturesque and friendly country is made only more beautiful during this annual celebration as locals don their best summer outfits; put flowers in their hair; stay outside all day long; and feast on traditional Swedish dishes like salmon, potatoes, and fresh strawberry cake.

## Ride a Gondola in Venice

There's possibly no bucket list item more inherently romantic than taking a gondola ride in Venice, Italy, and sharing a kiss under the Bridge of Sighs. While some might call it overdone, it's a once-in-a-lifetime activity and a beautiful way to see the city. Plus, with rising global water levels, we can't be sure how much longer gondola rides through the canals of Venice will be an option at all. For now, bring cash and hire a gondolier on the spot to row you through the scenic canals. There are different areas to enter the canals, with the most trafficked being the Grand Canal. Instead, walk a bit farther to experience a gondola ride in the quieter neighborhood canals, which will feel more peaceful and authentic (even if the activity is really just for tourists now).

## Experience the Soul of Seoul

World-class restaurants and an emphasis on communal dining experiences make a trip to Seoul, South Korea, perfect for group travelers. Experience cooking your own meal at your table with Korean barbecue and then eating family-style—and that's only round one of eating for the night. The Korean tradition of eating in rounds means that after dinner you may stop by the bar for beer and snacks, and only after that do you have dessert! Besides the incredible food scene, Seoul is also considered one of the best cities for nightlife. In neighborhoods like Hongdae or Itaewon, the party never seems to stop. If you're looking for something more low-key, try heading to a pocha—a casual tented drinking spot on the street where you can meet young, social locals. If you're looking for an icebreaker, ask some friendly locals to show you Korean drinking games.

# INDEX

## About the Author

**AUSTA SOMVICHIAN-CLAUSEN** is a multihyphenate living in New York City. Her work has appeared in publications such as *Thrillist, InsideHook, The Hill, Apartment Therapy, National Geographic, Women's Health,* and more. A dual citizen and proud member of the AAPI and LGBTQ+ communities, Austa is a dynamic creative with a deep love of travel, culture, and the environment.